WITHDRAWN

Carolyn G. Heilbrun

Twayne's United States Authors Series

Frank Day, Editor

Clemson University

TUSAS 672

CAROLYN G. HEILBRUN.
© *Joel Levin*

Carolyn G. Heilbrun

Julia B. Boken

State University of New York, College at Oneonta

Twayne Publishers
An Imprint of Simon & Schuster Macmillan
New York

Prentice Hall International
London   Mexico City   New Delhi   Singapore   Sydney   Toronto

Selections from Carolyn G. Heilbrun's work reprinted by permission of Carolyn G. Heilbrun.

Twayne's United States Authors Series No. 672

Carolyn G. Heilbrun
Julia B. Boken

Twayne Publishers
An Imprint of Simon & Schuster Macmillan
1633 Broadway
New York, New York 10019

Library of Congress Cataloging-in-Publication Data

Boken, Julia B.
    Carolyn G. Heilbrun / Julia B. Boken.
       p.   cm. — (Twayne's United States authors series ; TUSAS 672)
    Includes bibliographical references and index.
    ISBN 0-8057-4030-9 (alk. paper)
    1. Heilbrun, Carolyn G., 1926–   —Criticism and interpretation.
  2. Detective and mystery stories, American—History and criticism.
  3. Feminism and literature—United States—History—20th century.
  4. Women and literature—United States—History—20th century.
  5. Criticism—United States—History—20th century. 6. Fansler,
  Kate (Fictitious character) I. Title. II. Series.
    PS3558.E4526Z58   1996
    813'.54—dc20   96–20002
                                            CIP

10 9 8 7 6 5 4 3 2 1

Printed in the United States of America

In loving memory of Stephanie Boken, my mother,
and Anne Boken, my sister,
strong and courageous women who taught me
how to live and how to die

And to Dr. Maxine Theodoulou, psychologist and general semanticist,
my intelligent, witty, and unconditionally accepting friend,
who always listens, often advises, and never moralizes

Contents

Preface

The purpose of *Carolyn G. Heilbrun* is to present a long-overdue study of a multifaceted and innovative professor/writer who merged her training in English literature and criticism with her abiding interest in feminism to become a path-breaking scholar in the study of women in literature. Unlike most literature professors, Heilbrun is also a writer of detective fiction. In her eleven mystery novels, Heilbrun, writing under the pseudonym Amanda Cross, draws from her academic background to create her own woman in literature: a college professor who in the course of solving all kinds of mysteries—literary as well as criminal—illuminates numerous social, cultural, and feminist concerns. Heilbrun's courage in taking this road little traveled by academics translates for many critics into an image of her as a woman writing her own script instead of society's (that is, defining her own values and processing them without regard to the male point of view). *Carolyn G. Heilbrun* delineates the genesis and development of a woman who has carved her own path.

I begin by presenting the major influences and experiences that formed Heilbrun: her forebears, her education, and her struggle to achieve in a male-dominated academic universe, all of which led to her eventual triumph in becoming a respected scholar and to her exploration of the treatment of women in fiction. All such formative influences notwithstanding, Heilbrun once declared that she "was born a feminist." This opening chapter lays bare the underpinnings of the devotion to the empowerment of women that has come to dominate Heilbrun's work.

In chapter 2, I examine Heilbrun's early scholarly works: two biographies and an album. *The Garnett Family* (1961) emerged from her dissertation at Columbia University. This book presents the history of a literary family of librarians, editors, and writers and marks the beginning of Heilbrun's promising career in literary historical analysis. Her next book in this genre is the monograph *Christopher Isherwood* (1971), which depicts the life of a writer acknowledged to be among the best British novelists of his generation. Thus demonstrating her continued interest in prominent literary figures, Heilbrun focuses on Isherwood's artistic integrity as he illuminates through fiction important tensions of his time, especially in *Berlin Stories,* which many critics agree constitutes the best account of Hitler's nascent dictatorship. The final work discussed in this chapter is *Lady Ottoline's Album* (1976). It focuses on Violet Anne Cavendish-Bentinck (1873–1938), also known as Lady Ottoline, idiosyncratic woman of advanced views and aesthete extraordinaire, who presided over a Bohemian circle attracting T. S. Eliot, Virginia Woolf, and D. H. Lawrence, among others. The "album" is a collection of photographs taken primarily by Lady Ottoline—who was also an accomplished photographer—of luminaries in the Bloomsbury group. Heilbrun appends commentary on these famous men and women, who in their novels, poems, biographies, and criticism shaped the literary landscape of their generation.

Chapter 3 is devoted to Heilbrun's early feminist writings, *Toward a Recognition of Androgyny* (1973) and *Reinventing Womanhood* (1981). In the first book Heilbrun explores her ideal of "androgyny" (in which a person has a balance of male and female characteristics, with no rigid assignment of traits according to gender). The author plumbs the hidden river of androgyny in mythology and early literature and discusses the woman as hero in the novels of Samuel Richardson, Jane Austen, George Eliot, Henry James, and others. She also evaluates the significance of the Bloomsbury group's rejection of male-female stereotypes. Here as elsewhere in this volume, a discussion of Heilbrun's work is followed by a variety of critical views that appeared at the time in response to the book. *Reinventing Womanhood* is examined in light of Heilbrun's belief that women, by means of a raised consciousness, must reinvent themselves, redefine themselves, retell their life stories as they perceive them, not as they have been scripted by the traditional, male-dominated culture.

In chapters 4 and 5, I discuss the widely known and translated Amanda Cross detective novels. Chapter 4 considers the five novels published from 1964 to 1976, chapter 5 the remaining six, concluding with Heilbrun's latest novel to date, *An Imperfect Spy,* which appeared in 1995. These two chapters summarize the books and limn the protagonist/ sleuth Kate Fansler, along with her championing of basic, positive values in a flawed universe, her efforts to combat evil, and her rejection of stereotyped sex roles. All of the Amanda Cross novels express Heilbrun's fervent feminism and condemn the destructive hegemony of patriarchy.

Carolyn Heilbrun's later, specifically feminist works are explored in chapter 6, along with a book she edited with Margaret R. Higonnet, *The Representation of Women in Fiction* (1981). This book contains a selection of papers given at the annual meeting of the English Institute, a conference that attracts scholars in literature throughout the United States. At this first institute meeting devoted to feminist criticism, speakers presented papers on Jane Austen, Katherine Mansfield, Virginia Woolf, and George Sand. In *Writing a Woman's Life* (1988), now virtually a classic in women's studies, Heilbrun calls on women to consider new options and to forge their own destinies by not making men the center of their lives. Picking up on ideas she raised in *Reinventing Womanhood,* she urges women to write their own narratives, that is, to use their criteria—not men's—in writing biography, autobiography, and other genres. This chapter also includes an analysis of *Hamlet's Mother* (1990), a collection of essays in which Heilbrun explores several topics, mostly revolving around feminism and women in literature. The final book examined in this chapter is *The Education of a Woman: The Life of Gloria Steinem* (1995), a biography of the nationally known feminist. Heilbrun presents a sympathetic portrait of Steinem's life and work as a feminist, political activist, journalist, and cofounder of *Ms.* magazine.

Acknowledgments

I wish to thank—

Patrick Meanor, worthy and sensitive colleague, who, among all the arts, particularly enriched my perceptions of music—that wondrous handmaiden of literature—and who extended (as always) his generous advice in the writing of this book.

Dean James Mullen, Professor of Art and Dean of the Humanities and Fine Arts, State University of New York, College at Oneonta, for his academic and personal support in all of my woe and joy.

The library staff at Columbia University and at the State University of New York, College at Oneonta, particularly Janet Potter and Kay Benjamin. Both libraries have been of invaluable help in obtaining information and materials in the preparation of this book.

Dr. Jeffery Osterman, chiropractor, who during the writing of this book provided postsurgical care and who cheered me on.

Cheryl Peeters, whose typing and editing skills were of high quality and whose superefficiency, intelligence, and energy were indispensable in the production of this book.

Margaret Sanchez for her multidirectional help.

Grace Shultis, secretary to the Department of English, State University of New York, College at Oneonta, who through the years has made life on campus doubly enjoyable.

Frank Day and Mark Zadrozny for their helpful assistance, especially India Koopman for her keenly perceptive and intelligent editing, and Andrew Libby for his well-focused final-stage editing and his kind, gentle words.

Chronology

1973   *Toward a Recognition of Androgyny.* Becomes member of editorial board, *Twentieth Century Literature.*

1974   Teaches at Yale University.

1975   Appointed to editorial board, *Signs* magazine (serves through 1979).

1976   Editor, *Lady Ottoline's Album. The Question of Max* (as Amanda Cross). Elected to executive council, Modern Language Association (MLA; serves through 1979). Awarded Rockefeller Foundation Humanities Fellowship. Becomes Fellow of the Radcliffe Institute for Independent Study. Founding president, *Virginia Woolf Society* (serves through 1978).

1977   Elected to advisory board, *University of Michigan Press Series on Women and Culture.*

1978   Joins policy advisory council, Danforth Graduate Fellowship Program (serves through 1980).

1979   *Reinventing Womanhood.* Visiting professor, University of California, Santa Cruz.

1980   Becomes member of supervising committee, English Institute (serves through 1983).

1982   *Death in a Tenured Position* (as Amanda Cross). Teaches at Princeton University. Serves on advisory board, Institute for Research on Women, Rutgers University, New Jersey. Joins executive council, MLA (serves through 1984).

1983   Editor, *The Representation of Women in Fiction.* Joins advisory board, Project on Women and Social Change, Smith College, Massachusetts. Named as National Endowment for the Humanities Senior Fellow for Independent Study and Research Fellowship.

1984   *Sweet Death, Kind Death* (as Amanda Cross). Wins Wellesley College Alumnae Achievement Award. Elected president MLA.

1985   Appointed Avalon Foundation Professor in the Humanities at Columbia University.

1986   *No Word from Winifred* (as Amanda Cross). Becomes first director of Columbia University's Institute for Research on Women and Gender.

Chapter One
The Life of an Outsider

"I had been born a feminist"

No woman in the American academic world has mapped out as consistent a use of literature in her work—in literary criticism, literary biography, feminist writings, and detective fiction—as Carolyn G. Heilbrun. Although most often limiting her focus to modern British literature, Heilbrun has read and explored many other literatures as well. Her creative life is a virtual paradigm of the people, literary periods, genres, and themes she has favored in her pursuit of scholarly research and publication. From her scholarly work to her detective stories, Heilbrun's thematic interests seem to stem from her need to break away from limitations: those placed on women by Judaism, her ancestors' religion (abandoned by her parents); those placed on Jews by mainstream American culture; and those placed on women in private and in public life, especially, for Heilbrun, in academia, embodied for her in Columbia University, where she taught for 33 years. Those things Heilbrun most values, as expressed in all of her writing, are education, literature, freedom for women, wit, justice, and the eternal search for comity. As will be seen in this brief biography, her work mirrors her life.

Early Years

Parentage   Carolyn Gold was born 13 January 1926 in East Orange, New Jersey, the only child of Archibald and Estelle Gold. Her father, the youngest child of Hirsh Gold and Rebecca Engel, was born in Latvia, then a province of czarist Russia. Archibald's father died in Russia, but his mother emigrated to the United States along with him and his siblings. Carolyn Gold's mother, Estelle Roemer, was born in Manhattan, daughter of Austrians Samuel Roemer and Sadie Rosenzweig.

Archibald Gold's story is the virtual fulfillment of the American dream. He learned English, although his mother never did, and to earn money even taught his adopted language to older men. Although he later became a millionaire, his early years were impoverished. Carolyn

Heilbrun, reading Irving Howe's *World of Our Fathers* years later, saw in the book the history of her father's difficult life after his arrival in the New World. As he had in Europe, Gold scorned belief in Judaism, which his mother still practiced. In years to come, although Archibald Gold would take time off for the High Holidays, he and his family would never become practicing Jews. In fact, the Golds in the 1930s joined the "Divine Science" Church of the Healing Christ, whose pastor was Emmet Fox, a well-known preacher.

Estelle Roemer Gold was the eldest of seven children. Heilbrun writes that her maternal grandmother, Sadie, "impaired her six daughters for autonomy as thoroughly as if she had crippled them—more so. The way to security was marriage."[1] The young Carolyn most certainly felt even then the need for autonomy, a factor that likely drew her to and shaped her future views on feminism. Her grandmother Sadie persisted in her belief in Judaism and kept a kosher household until her death. Estelle was the only one of the family who refused to follow the Jewish faith. Heilbrun also alludes to her mother's frustration over the imprisoning conditions of her gender, which were common to the women of her generation. She told her daughter Carolyn, "Be independent, make your own way, do not pay with your selfhood for male admiration and approval: the price is too high" (*RW*, 17).

Archibald Gold, like most Russian Jews, suffered from virulent anti-Semitism in his home country, and Heilbrun writes of her father's disaffection from his ethnic roots. "He was early disenchanted with the whole culture from which he had come, with its ignorance, its illiteracy, and what he early considered its rigid, distorted beliefs" (*RW*, 21). Despite making a number of allusions to her forebears, Heilbrun virtually disdains interest in her European roots. "My lack of interest in my own roots was absolute and this was not a pretense. As far as I could see, my parents' roots consisted precisely in their severing of them. . . . My father had been his own creation" (*RW*, 19).

Gold, like many impecunious but ambitious immigrants, attended college at night; he developed proficiency in mathematics, graduated, and became a certified public accountant. In time he advanced to partnership in a brokerage firm and in the early 1930s became a millionaire. The Golds moved to the Upper West Side of Manhattan in 1932, but the Great Depression caught up with them the following year, and Archibald lost his fortune. When the head of his brokerage firm suffered a heart attack, Gold himself collapsed psychically. Now there was no money, and he was jobless. He then began more than two years of psychoanalysis and forever after admired Freud. (Perhaps as a result, Heilbrun herself has an affinity for Freud, although she, like many feminists, has some misgivings about the Austrian father of psychoanalysis.) Eventually, Gold recovered his psychic balance, returned to accounting, and again amassed a healthy fortune, finally buying an apartment on Fifth Avenue. After rebuilding his fortune he retired. Years later, in 1985, Archibald Gold died in Florida.

While her husband did acknowledge his Jewish heritage by observing the High Holidays, Estelle Roemer Gold remained opposed to Judaism her entire life in every respect. "From an early age," Heilbrun writes, "my mother identified all that limited her life as Judaism" (*RW*, 57). She had wished to become a nurse, but her orthodox mother forbade her to enter training and insisted that her only option was marriage. Heilbrun's mother believed Gentiles were able to enjoy life more than Jews. Although she never finished high school, Estelle Roemer did attend secretarial school and eventually became a skilled stenographer, working only until she married Archibald Gold at the age of 23. Estelle Gold died in Manhattan in 1973.

Childhood and education   Given that both of her parents showed their independence by breaking away from ethnic and religious traditions, it is perhaps not surprising that Carolyn Heilbrun developed a keen sense of independence and set off to forge her own destiny or, as she might say, to write her own script. As she grew up, Carolyn Gold attended private elementary and secondary schools in Manhattan. All of this special schooling, coupled with that of college and university, combined to give her a background in literature that would become a sine qua non in the development of her ideas—feminist and otherwise. An omnivorous reader from her childhood, she haunted the St. Agnes branch of the New York Public Library in the 1930s and 1940s. Preferring biographies, she raced through the library's collection in alphabetical order, reading largely the life stories of men because of the paucity of biographies by and about women.[2] Eventually, this lack of biographies of women would influence her work, leading to the publication of *Writing a Woman's Life* and her biography of Gloria Steinem. The voracious reading of Heilbrun's early adolescent years included the popular Nancy Drew and Judy Bolton mystery novels, perhaps prefiguring her later interest in writing mysteries herself under the pseudonym Amanda Cross.

During her early teenage years, Heilbrun also began reading the novels of Willa Cather and Virginia Woolf, that English feminist writer who profoundly affected Heilbrun's thinking on feminism and her scholarly writings. Heilbrun eventually served as editor of the *Virginia Woolf Newsletter* and was founding president of the Virginia Woolf Society.

Carolyn Gold attended Wellesley College in Massachusetts, an all-women's school, during 1944–47. There, as she told an interviewer, "Everybody was blond and WASP and Republican and didn't have, as far as I could see, a thought about anything except getting engaged.[3] These disparaging remarks notwithstanding, as an undergraduate she herself married the Manhattan-born James Heilbrun, then a Harvard student. They married near the end of World War II in 1945, on the eve of James's departure to the Pacific. Later in life she would call this still-intact marriage of more than 50 years "probably the single, most fortunate factor in my life" (*RW*, 17). For a long time she tried to keep her early marriage at 19 a secret, not wanting to be seen as a role model for young women considering the same.

At Wellesley she majored in literature and philosophy. Concerning her years there, Heilbrun reproves her alma mater for being "marvelously uncommitted to the problems of women in our time" (*RW*, 18). She also criticized Wellesley for having been, "in the nicest way, anti-Semitic." She began to see this anti-Semitism as being significant to her feminism years later, in 1976–77, while at the Radcliffe Institute for Independent Study in Cambridge, Massachusetts. "I began to understand that having been a Jew, however unobservable that identification was, however fiercely I denied the adamant anti-Semitism all around me as I grew up—still, having been a Jew had made me an outsider. It had permitted me to be a feminist" (*RW*, 20). Returning from a trip to Wellesley, she remembers telling the dean of the Radcliffe Institute, "I had always assumed that Wellesley ignored me because I was a feminist. Now, I had discovered, Wellesley had ignored me because I was a Jew. . . . The significance for me of that moment, only later recognized, was that for the first time, the two terms had come together: feminist and Jew" (*RW*, 18–19).

Heilbrun never complained about the quality of education she received at Wellesley, however. In 1947 she graduated Phi Beta Kappa with majors in English and philosophy. After graduation she worked for a short time in radio and publishing, experiences that gave her some useful exposure to the world outside cloistered academia, where she would spend most of her life. Soon thereafter she abandoned these jobs to enter graduate school at Columbia University, where she completed work for a master of arts degree in 1951 and a Ph.D. in 1959, concentrating on modern British literature. This literature—especially the work of Virginia Woolf, T. S. Eliot (considered English as well), E. M. Forster, Vanessa Bell, and Lytton Strachey—would become the hallmark of her writing; she would weave her knowledge of these writers and modern British literature into her understanding of feminism and of critical theory concerning women and biography.

Heilbrun's first teaching job, at Brooklyn College, lasted one year. Immediately after, in the fall of 1960, she taught modern British literature at Columbia University, beginning a life-long affiliation. In 1963 James Heilbrun returned to graduate school, and by this time the Heilbruns had three children, all under the age of eight: Emily, Margaret, and Robert.

Career at Columbia

At Columbia University Carolyn Heilbrun advanced from instructor (1960–62) to assistant professor (1962–67)—receiving a Guggenheim Fellowship in 1967—then to associate professor (1967–72). Finally, in 1972, she became tenured and a full professor. During these 12 years of rising through the academic ranks, Heilbrun published a number of books. First was *The Garnett Family* (1961), a historical study of the famous English family that produced librarians, editors, writers, and translators and who befriended many rising luminaries of British literature. Her first two Amanda Cross novels, *In the Last Analysis* (1964) and *The James Joyce Murders* (1967), were published while she was teaching full-time, and they were soon followed by *Christopher Isherwood* (1970) and her third and fourth Amanda Cross novels, *Poetic Justice* (1970) and *The Theban Mysteries* (1971). Also during those years, she became an honorary fellow of the American Association of University Women and editor of the *Virginia Woolf Newsletter* and was elected to the editorial board at Columbia University Press. These and other accomplishments testify to Carolyn Heilbrun's high level of activity not only in publishing but also in literary associations, yardsticks that Columbia University has always used to measure those faculty worthy of retention, promotion, and merit increases. Heilbrun, however, laments that her full professorship was belated by any standard.

As Heilbrun wrote books and taught at colleges around the country, she became affiliated with powerful literary and feminist organizations and magazines and was given accolades that catapulted her to the national forefront. Following the publication of *Toward a Recognition of*

Androgyny in 1973, she was during the balance of the 1970s appointed to the editorial board of *Signs,* a prestigious magazine of literary criticism; elected to the executive council of the Modern Language Association; awarded fellowships from the Rockefeller Foundation and from the Radcliffe Institute for Independent Study; and became founding president of the Virginia Woolf Society.

Her teaching at the University of California at Santa Cruz and at Princeton University during the late 1970s and early 1980s exposed her to a wide range of feminist women and ideas. At this juncture of her life, Heilbrun begins to develop a keener sensibility as to the problems and issues concerning women and feminism. She will still use literature in her writings, but it will be the handmaiden to feminism. Through such great exemplars as Virginia Woolf, Jane Austen, and Vanessa Bell and such contemporary writers as Adrienne Rich and Audre Lord, Heilbrun wrote of the feminism of women with indisputable literary talents. At this time she also joined the Policy Advisory Council of the Danforth Fellowship program and became a member of the supervising committee for the English Institute, a group attracting academics annually to hear one another speak on a variety of scholarly subjects. (As mentioned in the preface, this affiliation led to her editing of *The Representation of Women in Fiction,* published in 1981.)

Because of her increasingly high profile in feminist studies, women's institutes around the country vied for her support, and she was appointed to the most elite groups formed around women's issues, such as the University of Michigan Series on Women and Culture, which is devoted to publishing books on feminism in the academy, feminist poetry and theory, and sexual politics in various countries throughout the world. In 1986 Heilbrun became Columbia University's first director of the Institute on Research on Women and Gender, which concerns itself with interdisciplinary teaching and scholarship, organizing seminars, conferences, lectures, and research projects on feminism and gender studies.

After the publication of *Lady Ottoline's Album* in 1976, Heilbrun wrote *Reinventing Womanhood* (1979), *Writing a Woman's Life* (1988), and the essays collected in *Hamlet's Mother and Other Women* (1990). These three scholarly books on women and literature and feminism, along with Heilbrun's *Toward a Recognition of Androgyny,* display her wide range of reading and erudition and her desire to put them in the service of feminism. Although, as mentioned, her special field is modern British literature, she has used the literature of many literary and cultural periods to write of androgyny—man in woman and woman in man. Conversant with an enormous range of literature—biblical, Renaissance, Shakespearean, eighteenth-, nineteenth-, and twentieth-century American, British, and Continental—she has made from her knowledge a banner to urge women to fight for freedom, to avoid sexual polarization, and to engender their empowerment. Heilbrun issues a clarion call, asking women to reinvent womanhood by rejecting dependency on men. Not like the firebrands who led or accompanied men in the French Revolution, Heilbrun, echoing Simone de Beauvoir in *The Second Sex*, instead uses rationality, wit, and wisdom to encourage women to write their own narratives through biography and autobiography and to accept neither the definition of feminism nor the limitation of female experience as understood by men.

These Heilbrun writings, too, underscore the importance of feminist criticism in literary studies, since literary criticism by men has virtually ignored the role and significance of women in literature. In *Writing a Woman's Life*, she declares, "We know we are without a text and must discover one" (*WWL*, 44). Heilbrun in her scholarly books designed a new frame for the interpretation of Hamlet's mother and Virginia Woolf, Penelope in *The Odyssey*, feminism, and the profession of literature. She also wove into several of these four books her attitudes and experiences about reading and writing detective novels. Often, in essays about literature and research, Heilbrun also discusses detective stories. This is especially so in *Hamlet's Mother*, in the chapter "The Detective Novel of Manners," where she discusses *Gaudy Night* as Dorothy Sayers's most feminist novel; Heilbrun thus merges her interest in literature, detective novels, and feminism. Throughout her work Heilbrun also discusses the skill the detective and the literary researcher must possess: the ability to ferret out facts and make sense of them. (Between 1976 and 1995 Heilbrun published seven more Amanda Cross novels, bringing the total to 11.)

The Significance of Lionel Trilling

Carolyn Heilbrun's tenure at Columbia University has many modalities, but during her teaching years she assumed a high profile nationally, a development especially significant for feminism, for literature, and for the academy throughout the nation. Here it seems most relevant to address her relations with the late Lionel Trilling, her one-time teacher and later colleague in the Department of English and Comparative

Literature, who is still considered to have been one of Columbia's most distinguished professors.

Lionel Trilling was a profound influence on Heilbrun's literary perceptions. To assert her gratitude to Trilling as her professor, Heilbrun quotes William Gibson's remark in *A Season of Heaven:* that in every fortunate life, "there is one teacher that places a finger upon the soul"[4] (*RW,* 126). For her, Lionel Trilling was that teacher, despite his predilection for male students.

In the 1960s, when Heilbrun came to teach in the Department of English and Comparative Literature, she was among the vanguard of women teachers at Columbia. Trilling was visibly disturbed when women were hired for the first time at Columbia College, an undergraduate division. He is reported to have said: "This is not at all a good idea," and then added, "Older men should teach younger men and younger men should then go out and encounter women as the Other" (Matthews, 73). Many of Trilling's students have attested to his penchant for a small coterie of male students. In a long discussion about Trilling in *Reinventing Womanhood* (125–38), Heilbrun recalls that he was oblivious to her adulation; in fact, she does not mention the existence of even a surface relationship between Professor Trilling and herself as graduate student. Despite this lack of mutual acknowledgment and despite Heilbrun's reservations about his views on women—in life and in literature—she pays tribute over and over again to Lionel Trilling. Even though he found in her a person "whose cultural attitudes he couldn't admire" (*RW,* 126–27), Heilbrun acknowledged that he deeply touched her life.

When Heilbrun became his colleague at Columbia, Trilling maintained a psychic distance. "During all the years we were colleagues," she writes, "he never once talked to me," except in some courteous exchange (*RW,* 127). Trilling knew of her immersion in the study of women in literature, and his bias against such study might have been one reason for his distance. Heilbrun writes, without expressly indicting Trilling, "As far as I know he never took the opportunity to comment on what might be called the feminine revolution without disparaging it, seeing in it profound dangers to the proud, masculine life" (*RW,* 129). Had they had any discourse, Heilbrun further states that even though he taught her most of what she was "to learn about the connection between literary ideas and culture," she would have wanted "to let him know that the anger of women, wholly displaced from power, was also a cultural fact" (*RW,* 127–28).

In 1975 Trilling died from cancer. Ironically, sometime before his demise, Heilbrun had been solicited to substitute for the ailing Trilling in giving the annual address to the Friends of the Columbia Libraries. She accepted, and her speech, concerning women and biography, a theme Trilling would not have approved, was given on the very day he succumbed (*RW,* 127–28).

Eight years after Trilling's death, in 1983, Columbia College became the last of the Ivy League schools to turn coed. In this stronghold of male control, Carolyn Heilbrun had begun her teaching. Like many universities in the United States then, there were more men than women on faculties, more tenured men, and more men promoted to higher academic ranks. Even today the balance still tips in favor of men.

Feminism

Carolyn Heilbrun once wrote, "I had been born a feminist," but she does not elaborate (*RW,* 16). One can intuit, though, that early in her life, especially given her family's free thinking and its opposition to the Judaic strictures of her grandmothers, she was determined not to follow in the wake of her mother, who by virtue of the family and the era she was born into had been unable to establish her own career. Carolyn Heilbrun admits that even in her age group she is one of the few women who are feminists. "What becomes evident in studying women like myself," she writes, "women who moved against the current of their times, is that some condition in their lives insulated them from society's expectations and gave them a source of energy, even a sense of destiny, which would not permit them to accept the conventional female role. Some condition of being a outsider gave them the courage to be themselves" (*RW,* 30).

Because feminism is so central to Heilbrun's identity and her work, it's important to be clear about what she understands it to be. There are dozens of definitions of feminism, but many feminists believe that a plurality of definitions may be healthy, barring no one who believes in the empowerment of women. Heilbrun favors the following definition of feminism, constructed by Nancy Miller in *Subject to Change* (1988): the wish "to articulate a self-consciousness about women's identity both as inherited cultural fact and as process of social construction" and to "protest against the available fiction of female becoming"[5] This passage, composed in a high level of abstraction, argues that women must be made aware that tradition and society (almost wholly controlled by men in the past) have fashioned the identity of women. Now women must design and articulate their own matrices in controlling their own emerging destiny.

In the 1970s feminism was becoming an academic industry, one of the themes in a *New York Times* interview of Carolyn Heilbrun by Ann Matthews. Matthews writes that although "Carolyn Heilbrun helped found academic feminism, she has always remained slightly apart, allied to no camp, entirely pleasing no one with her insistence that literature and life are linked, that we are the stories we tell."[6] Again, Heilbrun is shown to be an outsider.

Although Heilbrun seems not to have aligned herself with any specific faction of the feminist cause, Christina Hoff Sommers, a Clark University philosopher, in *Who Stole Feminism? How Women Have Betrayed Women*[7] defines some types of feminism that may help the reader to place Heilbrun. Sommers defines equity feminists as those who wish the same rights and privileges as men. She then defines as gender, or new, feminists those who wish to rewrite history, to have more rights than men to compensate for their past powerlessness, to wage war against men. Sommers classifies Gloria Steinem, Marilyn French, and Susan Faludi as gender feminists. Even in title their books unmistakably point to rage, to battle, to revolution.[8] It is no secret that Heilbrun has closely associated with these three women, among many others of similar category, as discussed in Sommers's book. Heilbrun also wrote a testimonial espousing rebellion for *The War against Women* by Marilyn French.

Retirement

After more than three decades on the faculty of Columbia University, Carolyn Heilbrun retired in 1992 at age 66 rather than the usual age of 70. She retired early, as she wrote and explained in interviews at the time, to protest maltreatment by her male colleagues, their lack of commitment to feminist studies, and their denial of tenure to several women. Heilbrun objected to the fact no women served on the tenure committee at this time. Clearly, her early retirement demonstrates the rebellion she had practiced over the course of many years; she was still the "outsider."

Although Carolyn Heilbrun once described her male colleagues as "the tree house gang," playing "in a tree house: No girls allowed,"[9] some professors in the Department of English and Comparative Literature take issue with her view. Professor George Stade, a veteran professor of the department, said, "It is hard for her to make a case for gross injustice. If we all have some deep anti-female prejudice, I can't see it myself. Professor Heilbrun has always been aggrieved, always" (Matthews, 75). Professor David Kasten, chair of the department, also objected to her negative assessment of the department concerning women and feminist studies. As reported in the *New York Observer,* he said, "I think Columbia, like many places, has seriously tried to add more women. I actually do believe that throughout the Department—I'm certain of this—that there is a real commitment to feminist scholarship."[10]

Yet Dr. Robert Manning concedes there have been problems in the department and empathizes with Heilbrun's frustration. "In some quarters, I would say that my department still has some problems with dealing with feminism as a discipline and with the whole issue of what constitutes our responsibilities" (Progrebin, 25). In the same article, he pays tribute to Heilbrun as a role model for women who would enter the academy.

Conclusion

The mention of Carolyn Heilbrun as teacher elicited mixed reactions from many students who did not wish to go on record, while others thought her refreshingly direct. In one seminar Heilbrun is reported to have tossed a book and shouted, "Tom Eliot, how can you say that, you jerk?" Because she is smart, principled, and witty she has been feared and loathed on campus by some fellow faculty members (Matthews, 75). As she grew older and saw her teaching career coming to an end, she likely embraced a sentiment of Dorothy Sayers, which she cited in the epigraph to *Writing a Woman's Life* (125): "Time and trouble will tame an advanced young woman, but an advanced old woman is uncontrollable by any earthly force."

Sayers, the renowned English mystery writer and intellectual, has in many respects been an intellectual model for Heilbrun, and nowhere is this as clear as in the work of Heilbrun's "other self," detective novelist Amanda Cross. Since these novels have been translated into all major European languages, in addition to Japanese and Russian, and printings have reached well over a million copies all over the world, many readers recognize the name Amanda Cross more readily than Carolyn Heilbrun.

With the writing of the Amanda Cross novels, Carolyn Heilbrun designed a cosmos of her own psychic space. Why, given her many professional and familial responsibilities, did Heilbrun feel compelled to write detective novels? She enumerates a number of reasons, principally that she craved a space of her own (*WWL,* 114). She also writes, "I sought to create an individual [Kate Fansler, her amateur sleuth] whose destiny offered more possibility than I could comfortably imagine for myself" (*WWL,* 114). Also, having exhausted the shelves of English detective novels (mainly those by Agatha Christie, Josephine Tey, and Dorothy Sayers, her favorite), Heilbrun decided to write her own.

Heilbrun, who is often queried about using a pseudonym, asserts that she had initially feared being penalized by department members who would condemn such writings as frivolous and subsequently deny her tenure. She also felt "that secrecy gave me a sense of control over my destiny that nothing else in my life, in those pre-tenure, pre-women's movement days, afforded" (*WWL,* 117). This secrecy was maintained for six years until some enterprising person ferreted out her identity through a copyright search.

Carolyn Heilbrun's notable achievements extend in many directions—a long-lasting marriage and motherhood, a teaching career of 33 years, multifold scholarly books and articles, and 11 detective novels. Yet, when she focuses on the capstone of her academic career, Heilbrun writes, "Were I to mention the most important achievement of my career then, it would be the discovery of women's friendships, friendships which reverberate in the world of events." She then adds, "It is that miracle I desire for women."[11] Heilbrun refers in her article "Silence and Women's Voices" to those years when the women's movement began to flourish and she began friendships with a wide variety of feminist intellectuals around the country, especially those immersed in feminism and literature.

Heilbrun retired at the zenith of her academic career, a doyenne with a sizeable following, especially of younger feminists. She is still engaged in feminism and in writing, and she plans to continue with the Amanda Cross novels. She has tried to write fiction without Kate Fansler, but found that it didn't work. This creation of Heilbrun's "other self" continues to mesmerize her.

Chapter Two
Early Biographical Writings

"Biography is another way to a novel"

The books discussed in this chapter begin with *The Garnett Family* (1961), a study detailing the lives and contributions of a remarkable English family who were active in the development of the English library system and had a significant impact on the literature of their day. The next is *Christopher Isherwood* (1970), a monograph on the early work of an English writer who became one of the most respected and significant novelists of his generation. The chapter concludes with a discussion of *Lady Ottoline's Album* (1976), which is a collection of photographs, almost all taken by Lady Ottoline, a literary salon hostess known primarily for her connection with the Bloomsbury group, whose stamp on literature changed the contour of writing in England. In compiling the book Heilbrun selected quotations by and about these men and women to complement the original photographs. All three works are obvious expressions of her deep interest in modern British literature.

The Garnett Family

In 1961, one year after Carolyn Heilbrun joined the faculty of Columbia University, she published *The Garnett Family,* a book based on her Ph.D. dissertation.[1] This first book focuses on a notable bourgeois English family of several generations whose multifarious contributions to the literary world would reverberate for many years to come. In the annals of the history and development of library science, the younger Richard (1835–1906) became a quintessential figure in the development of the Library of the British Museum. Beyond these special contributions to the library, Richard Garnett and then his son Edward (1868–1937) advised, inspired, and nurtured many literary writers, with Edward being active in editing and otherwise aiding in the publication of writers such as Joseph Conrad, John Galsworthy, W. H. Hudson, and D. H. Lawrence, among many other men who would become famous in belles lettres. Carolyn Heilbrun also includes in this book a study of the work of

Constance Garnett (1862–1946), wife of Edward, and one of the first world-renowned translators of Russian literature into English.

The younger Richard Garnett, son of the elder Reverend Richard Garnett, started work with the library early in his life. Only a teenager when his father died, Richard, already respected for his learning and intellectual gifts, received offers of financial assistance from friends and relatives to prepare for and then attend Oxford or Cambridge University. He declined the offers for several reasons. For one, he felt the educational level of these now-prestigious universities was not adequate; he saw the chief benefits of attending as being social and material gain. Like his father, he abhorred advantage based on this kind of snobbery. Thus, in 1851, two days after his sixteenth birthday, he began working as an assistant in the Library of the British Museum, a career that was to extend for almost a half century (*GF,* 43). With no formal education beyond his sixteenth year, throughout his entire life Garnett became a legend for his extraordinary memory and for his fluency in Greek, Latin, French, German, Italian, Spanish, and other foreign languages. He read omnivorously and shared his erudition with people in Europe and America, becoming famous throughout the Western world.

Portrayed as a charismatic figure by Heilbrun, Richard Garnett helped the wealthy, the influential, and the poor—anyone who needed the library assistance that he could offer. Celebrated English writer Ford Maddox Ford comments on Garnett's sustained inclination to help all who came to the library: "It was an almost insoluble riddle that a personality so fine, so sardonic, so perceptive, should have given itself to the life of routine work that he led—that he should have allowed himself to be made a beast of burden for the cataloguers, the congresses, the questioners, and the editors of reviews."[2]

Heilbrun portrays Richard Garnett's intellectual and library achievements but makes comparatively little mention of his personal life—his marriage to Olivia Singleton, from an Anglo-Irish family of landowners in County Clare (*GF,* 43), and his progeny of six children, one of the most famous being Edward Garnett.

Richard Garnett's symbiosis with the Library of the British Museum ran concomitantly with the development of the modern library and with the emerging profession of librarianship. Thus readers will find this book informative as a limited history of the British Museum Library, interspersed with the biography of Richard Garnett, his son Edward, and Constance Garnett, Edward's wife. Under Richard Garnett's tenure, it became the largest library in the world (*GF,* 49). Yet, when he began his work there, because there was no catalogue of its collection, scholars and researchers were forced to travel to London to determine its holdings and acquisitions. In the 1880s, with Richard Garnett's encouragement, the printing of the *Catalogue* began. This Herculean undertaking was to continue for 25 years. By 1884, Garnett resigned from his position in the Reading Room, becoming chief editor of the *Catalogue;* six years later he became Keeper of the Printed Books, a position he held until his retirement in 1899 (*GF,* 50).

The *Catalogue,* representing the library's offerings as of the last day of the nineteenth century, finally saw the light of day in 1905. It remains a major accomplishment, being the first general catalogue of the British Museum Library, at that time one of the greatest of modern libraries, whose objects numbered 4.5 million (*GF,* 49).

Beyond Richard Garnett's exhaustive contributions to library service, which would benefit libraries everywhere, Heilbrun enumerates other benefactions by Garnett, including editing the *Selected Letters of Percy Bysshe Shelley,* noted English Romantic poet, and *Tales and Stories* by Mary Wollstonecraft Shelley, his second wife; writing countless articles for the *Encyclopedia Britannica;* organizing international library conferences (chiefly one in 1877, a convocation that led to the formation of the Library Association); and producing many biographies and critical writings on Milton, Dryden, Blake, Carlyle, and Edward Gibbon. Added to this array of publications are translations from Dante, Petrarch, and Camoëns. Gibbon also collaborated in the writing of a four-volume history of English Literature (*GF,* 57–59).

Additionally, as an avid reader of the work and the scholarship of William Shakespeare, Garnett wrote a drama in blank verse based on old tales of the Bard of Avon's purported arrest for poaching, his teaching, and his shrew of a wife entitled *William Shakespeare Pedagogue and Poacher.* He also published a volume of aphorisms on love, which he called *De Flagello Myrteo,* "after a sprig of myrtle planted by Shelley."[3]

Two books particularly highlighted by Carolyn Heilbrun are Richard Garnett's *Essays of an Ex-Librarian*[4] and his most famous novel, *The Twilight of the Gods,*[5] which Heilbrun cites as essentially pagan, mocking Christianity and all religions, yet with no spleen or bitterness. It is a collection of stories about the superseding of the gods by Christianity, a book that Heilbrun asserts is like nothing else in English literature: "religion, morality, learning and the conventions of civilization have been ridiculed" (*GF,* 64). Heilbrun believes the book is a classic—delightful in its satire, mocking man and his civilized attitudes but with an under-scoring of "gentle love for man's human goodness and the potency of his reason" (*GF,* 64). With *witchery* as a key word used by Heilbrun about this book, she concludes this segment on Richard Garnett the younger by commenting that he lived as if he existed apart from the constriction of Victorian struggle against religion, in its moral and social forms. He dedicated his life to learning and to sharing this knowledge with humankind. Richard Garnett's ultimate ideal recalls these lines in Tennyson's poem "Ulysses": "To follow knowledge like a sinking star / Beyond the utmost bounds of human thought." Charismatic and eru-dite, compassionate and generous and keeper of the flame of knowledge, Richard Garnett, concludes Heilbrun, "retained the best of the Victorian dream, and, mocking wittily at its moral and religious creeds, placed his faith in reason and the stars" (*GF,* 64).

Edward, the third of Richard Garnett's six children, veered off into a career somewhat different from that of his father. Distinguished for his enormous influence in the world of English literature, Edward Garnett, like all of his siblings, was surrounded by a rich literary environment from birth. Books were everywhere, literary personages whom Richard Garnett met through the British Library visited for tea, and, when Richard earned the title Keeper of Printed Books and was given housing next to the British Museum, the children played there. Like his father, Edward despised raw ambition, worldliness, and success. His formal education was limited, but he, like his father, read virtually unceasingly from 16 to 19 years of age. Although Edward Garnett did nothing but read, his father exerted no pressure on this son to follow a career. At the age of 20 he began working for the well-known publishing house of Unwin and eventually became a reader, a career perfectly suited to his character, his habits, and his tastes (*GF,* 70–71).

Carolyn Heilbrun writes, "For over forty years Edward Garnett had a powerful hand in much of the best that was written in English litera-ture" (*GF,* 66). Daily, as a reader, Garnett evaluated several novels, and if a writer were deemed talented, he would meet the novelist at a restau-rant or, in years to come, at his Chelsea flat, developing a mentoring relationship with the writer. Although Edward Garnett was no snob or cynic, he was known to favor the writer over the publisher and to deni-grate those who were obtuse about real talent and who instead fostered and read the mediocre, the sentimental, and the insincere, those Philistines that for him included academicians, publishers, reviewers, and the reading public. Heilbrun clearly emphasizes that Garnett in all his years of reading novels either handwritten or in typescript never missed a major talent except for James Joyce (*GF,* 67).[6]

For almost a decade, Edward Garnett continued to work for the publisher Unwin, honing his sharp critical ability. Heilbrun remarks that he discovered his niche and maintained his passion for reading talented artists and fostering their careers. She writes of him, "The monumental and selfless service he performed for English letters remains as evidence of an altruistic life" (*GF,* 71).

In 1889 he married Constance Black, several years older, with whom he had fallen almost immediately in love a few years before. Constance Garnett would become famous in her own right as a translator of many Russian novels and plays. Their only child, David, was born in 1892. Following his work at Unwin, Edward Garnett worked for several years at Heinemann's, another famous publishing company and then in 1901 he joined the firm of Gerald Duckworth. He signed up with the Friends Ambulance Corps in Italy during World War I, and then worked for the Jonathan Cape publishing company, a job he held until his death.

Always an outsider, Edward Garnett refused the C. H. (Companion of Honour), a highly esteemed title, and also turned down an honorary degree from the University of Manchester. Eccentric and irascible and fulminating against the Yahoos all of his adult life, Edward Garnett felt fulfilled only when dealing with writers of talent or genius. He picked up manuscripts at the office, spent a few days in London weekly, then rusticated at Cearne, his country house, near Edenbridge in Kent, where visitors included such future luminaries in English literature as D. H. Lawrence, Joseph Conrad, W. H. Hudson, and John Galsworthy as well as the American Stephen Crane. Heilbrun informs the reader that Garnett was the model for Bosinney in *The Forsyte Saga,* the famous novel by Galsworthy (*GF,* 78). Once finding a novelist he thought to be talented, Garnett read and evaluated his work, financially aided him, located lodging for him and generally cheered the writer on.

Although Garnett spent much of his time promoting promising writers, he also wrote and published his own: critical writings, novels, poems, plays, and articles on Icelandic sagas. According to Heilbrun, none of these is memorable. Often Galsworthy and Conrad read and made suggestions to Garnett on his work. Heilbrun discusses Garnett's published play *The Trial of Jeanne d'Arc* (1912) as flawed and compares this drama with George Bernard Shaw's highly successful and inspired play *Saint Joan.* D. H. Lawrence evaluated Garnett's play about the Maid of Orleans but apparently misunderstood many of its elements.

Heilbrun summons evidence that the coup de grace was struck at Garnett's theatrical career with the publication of the Shaw play (*GF*, 90), which was ignited by its political and sociological implications. Garnett was more successful in writing 22 satires against World War I, initially published in such leading magazines as the *Nation, Cambridge Magazine*, and the *English Review* and then collectively published in 1919 as *Papa's War and Other Stories,* Papa being the devil.[7]

In probing the oeuvre of Edward Garnett, Heilbrun asserts, that his "greatest editorial and critical work was done in the conversations, letters and comments he addressed to the writers whom he advised" (*GF*, 95). Another serious accomplishment concerned his almost weekly articles in *Speaker,* where he reviewed new novels, although many of these books are not at all remembered.

Surprisingly for this time, Edward Garnett supported many women writers, especially those who wrote of the struggle for women's rights. Garnett, says Heilbrun, believed "in complete female emancipation [and he] all of his life encouraged women writers and women artists" (*GF*, 100). Heilbrun further emphasizes that he was particularly effective in vigorously asserting women's rights and defending them along with the rights of men (*GF*, 101).

Most of the artists encouraged by Edward Garnett (excepting John Galsworthy) did not become successful until many years after Garnett's initial discovery of them, for example, Joseph Conrad, surprisingly, and W. H. Hudson. Heilbrun substantiates Joseph Conrad's debt to Garnett by her inclusion of a letter by Conrad to Edward's son. "Conrad maintained that Edward had made him an author. However much we may doubt the possibility of one man making an author of another, the relationship with Conrad provides one of the best examples of Garnett's talent in friendship and genius in criticism" (*GF*, 107). Conrad and Edward Garnett continued their frank, amicable, and intimate relationship for almost 30 years, until Conrad died in 1924.

Perhaps among the many contributions of Edward Garnett to literature, then, was his unalloyed support of talented but as yet unknown writers. Heilbrun believes that "with prose writers, Garnett's touch was all but infallible" (*GF*, 138). Heilbrun cites dozens of letters of gratitude from masters in English literature to Edward Garnett over the course of his nearly 60-year career. That Carolyn Heilbrun spent almost 100 pages on his life and work, the longest segment of *The Garnett Family,* attests to the significance she places on Edward Garnett's influence on English literature.

With Constance Garnett (1862–1946), the third major portrait in the book, Carolyn Heilbrun enters into her lifelong interest in the biography of women. She was born Constance Black, the sixth of eight children. Her grandfather Peter Black was naval architect to Tsar Nicholas I and was subsequently interred in the Russian naval fortress of Kronstadt. Constance's father, David, spent his formative years in Russia, returned to England, migrated to Canada, and then returned to England, working as a solicitor, becoming finally the coroner at Brighton.

Unlike the Garnetts—Richard and his son Edward—Constance Black was formally educated at Newnham College, Cambridge. Brilliant and charming, although often not in the peak of health, Constance won a scholarship to Newnham as the front-runner in a competition with more than 3,000 candidates from the south of England. For women at this time, university education, often considered a waste of time and counterproductive to the male's concept of sexuality, provided a challenge to the few who could brave the attendant obloquy. Despite their formal admission, women were forbidden to attend lectures at any of the university's colleges but Newnham; yet some famous male scholars duplicated or repeated their lectures for female students and even scheduled unusual laboratory hours for them, often for no salary.

When admitted in 1879, Constance Black, at 17, was the youngest woman in Newnham. At the end, she received the *equivalent* of a first-class degree. (According to Heilbrun, women were not granted titular degrees until 1921, but even these degrees "were, in fact, not proper degrees at all." Women were not permitted to become members of Cambridge University until 1947.) Jobs were limited even for brilliant women who were university graduates. Constance became a governess for younger girls and then a librarian. During this time she met Edward Garnett at his father's home and fell in love. They worked in the same Paternoster Row in London and began seeing each other daily.

Unlike the Garnetts, Constance became passionately absorbed in socialism, but in time believed that Karl Marx's theory of values in *Das Kapital*, as well as his economic interpretation of history, was flawed. By 1892, having met a number of Russian revolutionaries and exiles, she discarded Marx's theory of socialism (*GF*, 165). In 1893, though, she joined the Fabian Society, a socialist group founded in 1884 believing in a gradual rather than a revolutionary change in government. Among some habitués, Constance met George Bernard Shaw, the famous playwright, who said that he would have liked to marry her but could not afford to do so.

Edward and Constance married in 1889 and lived in the East End of London until 1891, when they left to live in Surrey to have a child. Their only child, David, was born in 1892. In Surrey, during her difficult recovery from childbirth, her life was to take a momentous turn when Edward brought home Felix Volkovsky, a Siberian escapee, broken in health, who suggested that Constance fill her hours studying Russian and left with her a Russian grammar, a dictionary, and a short story in Russian. Despite a number of health problems and the enormous difficulty of learning Russian, fluency in which can demand as many as 20 years of constant study, Constance, already having mastered Latin and Greek, further demonstrated her language proficiency and made rapid progress. Ivan Aleksandrovich Goncharov's "A Common Story" became her first Russian-English translation. It was accepted by Heinemann's and published in 1894. From that point on, for more than 30 years, the Russian translations virtually dominated her life. Turgenev and Chekhov were her favorites.

Always an independent spirit, Constance Garnett traveled to Italy alone to visit D. H. Lawrence and his wife, Frieda, and in 1894 she visited Russia, a remarkable feat for a woman traveling alone at that time. Her writing on that trip, set down 34 years later, still remains fresh and perceptive (GF, 179). The apogee of Garnett's trip to Russia undoubtedly came in meeting Count Leo Tolstoy at Yasnaya Polyana, his country estate, and dining with his family. In later years, when Garnett spent months translating Tolstoy's massive novel *War and Peace,* her eyesight, never strong, narrowly failed her. The novel was then read to her in Russian, and she dictated the English translation to an amanuensis. Her translation of *War and Peace* was published in London by Heinemann's in 1904.

On Constance Garnett's return from Russia in 1894 following her father's death, she received a legacy of £1,000. The Garnetts used this money to build a house in Cearne, where Constance remained for the rest of her days, with short intervals of travel and trips to London for David's education there. Despite her responsibilities as wife, mother, housekeeper, and hostess to the friends who visited Cearne, Garnett produced her translations with a remarkable speed and consistency. Her translation of *The Brothers Karamazov* by Fyodor Dostoyevsky was that novel's first into English. Of this time in Garnett's life, Carolyn Heilbrun writes, "It is a fact too little noticed that women of the middle or upper class have, through the centuries, done either so little or so much that one wonders, on the one hand, how they fill their days, on the other how their days are long enough" (GF, 181).

The English writer Arnold Bennett praised Constance Garnett for helping him through her translations in the craft or art of writing. He especially admired her translations of Chekhov's *Tales* and of Turgenev's *Fathers and Children,* published in the United States as *Fathers and Sons.* Heilbrun's appendix of Garnett's translations is—to any admirer of Russian literature read in English—an indication of her high level of productivity, a marvel in any age.

Heilbrun provides the reader of this book a most curious detail. In 1907, after having been turned down by the Scandinavian countries and by Finland, the Russian Social Democratic Party met in England. At this convention Constance Garnett met Lenin, Stalin, and Trotsky. She was asked to be Lenin's interpreter for a speech but declined, probably from shyness, although her formal reason was her inability to cope with Marxist terms in both languages.

Mrs. Garnett early concluded that the Bolsheviks were gangsters or crooks and felt no shred of sympathy for them, their revolution, or their experiment in communism. Heilbrun believes that Garnett's negative attitude toward communism saved her son, David, who had been romanticizing Marxism, from espousing this philosophy.

Constance Garnett would likely have been comfortable in our current age of multiculturalism; as Heilbrun comments, "She was until her death, inexhaustibly interested in foreign countries and foreign peoples, particularly the Chinese; she cherished the diversity of races, and dreaded a uniform way of life spreading over the globe" (*GF,* 183).

Garnett died at age 84 in Cearne, having left—as she herself estimated in the 35 years she translated Russian literature—approximately 70 volumes of work. Especially remarkable are such statistics as having translated 17 volumes of Turgenev, 13 volumes of Chekhov's *Tales,* a pair of volumes of his plays, 13 volumes of Dostoyevsky, 6 of Gogol, 4 of Tolstoy, and 6 of Herzen, the well-known Russian memoirist. (Her husband, Edward, wrote a number of introductions to his wife's translations, and a collection of those he wrote on her translations of Turgenev was published in 1917.[8]) Constance Garnett's obituary in the *New Republic,* quoted by Heilbrun, affirms her importance: "'Literally millions of American and English readers are indebted to her . . . for their first knowledge of a whole new world of fiction and drama'" (*GF,* 183).[9]

Heilbrun devotes a few pages in the "Constance Garnett" chapter to evaluating her translations, which she asserts were not always the first ones and not always the best. Still, the overall quality of her translations is attested to by many. Renowned Russian writer Maxim Gorky and

Lady Ottoline Morrell, for three decades a literary chatelaine (to be discussed later in this chapter), agreed on "the magnificence of Constance
Garnett's translations from the Russian."[10] Garnett's translations opened
a new and exotic world to many English-speaking readers.[11]

Heilbrun concludes her study of the Garnett family with a six-page
epilogue on Constance and Edward's son, David (1892–1981). Heilbrun
devotes little space to him because she believes his own memoirs in three
volumes[12] sufficiently cover his life. Heilbrun lauds the three-volume
work: "It relates in clear, unfaltering prose and with humour, intimacy
and charm, the attitude toward life of a literary generation" (GF, 197).
His portraits of members of the Bloomsbury group, including Vanessa
Bell, Virginia Woolf, and Logan Pearsall Smith, she states, will particularly intrigue devotees of English literature. David Garnett consorted
with the flamboyant "Bloomsberries," as they are sometimes called,
while flaunting his own conservative independence.

Initially, David Garnett trained for the biological sciences at the Royal
College of Science in South Kensington, but he soon abandoned this specialty for literature. In all, David Garnett wrote 11 novels. Heilbrun discusses the merit of these novels and comments, "In a David Garnett
novel, an event occurs, leading in turn to other events; there is no probing, however, into the psychological causes of action, nor into effects that
lie beyond the observed event." Influenced by Daniel Defoe, Garnett's
surreal, cerebral novel Lady into Fox[13]—which Heilbrun describes as his
first "in any meaningful sense"—became popular when it appeared in
the 1920s. In some of his novels, Garnett portrays his parents: his father
in Beany-Eye and as Roger in No Love, where his mother is depicted as
Alice (GF, 199).[14]

In his editing, translating, and writing, David Garnett carried on the
family tradition of intimate involvement with books. His column "Books
in General" appeared in the New Statesman and Nation from March 1933
to October 1939 (GF, 200), he published more than 30 books (including
the novels), and he edited, translated, or introduced dozens.

Heilbrun's statement regarding David Garnett's upbringing is revealing. "His parents brought him up remarkably free from the restrictions of
convention, the brutalization of schools, and the effeteness of universities"
(GF, 200). It is a telling commentary on some aspects of English society,
yet the reader would have liked a comment of such high density expanded.
Heilbrun asserts in her conclusion that in David Garnett's generation of
writers, including Virginia Woolf and D. H. Lawrence, English isolation
was overcome, religion lost its iron grip, and the power and prestige of

class privilege were lessened. Heilbrun's final comment in this collective biography is thought provoking: "Yet if the literature of England and Ireland flowered in David Garnett's generation, it was largely because past generations had made that flowering possible" (*GF*, 201).

The Garnett Family offers a number of portraits of an individualistic, untraditional, and independent family immersed in research, editing, publishing, translating, and writing. Heilbrun commands a familiarity with the English literature of the periods covered, and her book reflects accurate and thoughtful research.

One of the drawbacks of this book is that it lacks depth and drama. Richard Hoggart in *New Statesman* wrote that the many absorbing details do not attempt connections of depth or intricacy. "The individualist aesthetic, the intense personal responsibility, the sometimes arrogant anti-vulgarity, the reaction from bourgeois conventionalism—all are parts of that complex of attitudes which a book about the Garnetts should not fail to examine. Unfortunately, Miss Heilbrun does little more than make us realize that this is indeed what *should* be done."[15] Some readers, too, might have enjoyed a more compelling and a longer portrait of Constance Garnett, who was virtually a household name to those readers in the first half of the twentieth century familiar with Russian literature in translation.

These criticisms notwithstanding, *The Garnett Family* remains a useful guide to Constance Garnett's translations and to the novels and plays of Richard and Edward Garnett. Moreover, the many allusions in Heilbrun's book to the literary figures who were an integral part of the Garnetts' lives and who eventually became famous through the intercession of this eccentric and unusual family, especially by Edward Garnett, may be of interest not only to the neophyte but also to the sophisticated reader of English and comparative literature.

Christopher Isherwood

Carolyn Heilbrun's second publication, *Christopher Isherwood* (1970),[16] constitutes one of a series published under the aegis of the Columbia Essays on Modern Writers. With this essay she joined other well-known Columbia professors[17] in writing slim monographs on famous writers, hers amounting to 48 pages and numbered 53 in the series. Her subject, Christopher Isherwood, the British-born novelist and screenwriter, was 66 when Heilbrun's essay appeared. Isherwood died 16 years later, in 1986; by 1970 the bulk of his work had been published.

In this essay, Carolyn Heilbrun presents a brief biography of Isherwood. There is his father's death in World War I; public school at Repton, where he met W. H. Auden; his deliberate misbehavior, which caused him to be expelled from Cambridge; casual jobs; and medical school in 1928, which he abandoned after two semesters. Isherwood was then invited to join Auden, who would become a friend for life, in Berlin, Germany, a bohemian and intriguingly decadent city. There Isherwood met and had a homosexual affair with a German, Heinz.[18] Heilbrun does not mention the relationship because in the 1930s it was unacceptable to discuss or even mention *homosexuality*. The theme of homosexuality is nonetheless persistent in Isherwood's work. When the Nazis came to power in 1933, homosexuality was judged a serious offense. That same year Isherwood and Heinz left Berlin. They wandered throughout Europe until 1937, when Heinz was recalled to Germany, where Hitler's henchmen arrested him for homosexuality. In 1938 Isherwood traveled to China with Auden, and from that trip, in the first of several collaborations, the two wrote *Journey to a War*, about the Sino-Japanese conflict, published in 1939. When war between England and Germany loomed in 1939, Isherwood, obsessed with and dreading war and finding life impossible in England, left with Auden for the United States, where he remained for the rest of his life.

Isherwood settled in southern California, finding work in Hollywood. It was in California that he met Swami Prabhavananda, a Hindu monk, head of southern California's Vedanta Society. Isherwood subsequently accepted Vedantism, one of the orthodox systems of Indian philosophy, forming the nucleus of most modern schools of Hinduism. At one point he wished to become a monk.

Heilbrun gives token attention to Vedantism when she mentions Isherwood's *An Approach to Vedanta*, a pamphlet heavily influencing Isherwood's documentary-style novel *Down There on a Visit* (CI, 31–33), with its themes of the search for life's meaning and the constant failure of commitment. Irony is a weapon used against "Christopher," the dummy, as the writer simultaneously elicits from the reader compassion for and insight into two flawed men—an English homosexual and a young German man stung by English snobbery—among other characters.

Carolyn Heilbrun makes an important contribution in this essay by distinguishing two types of Isherwood novels. In the documentary-style novels—*The Last of Mr. Norris, Lions and Shadows, Journey to a War, Goodbye to Berlin, Prater Violet, The Condor and the Cows,* and *Down There on a Visit*—the character "Christopher Isherwood" appears, but the narrator, a ventriloquist's dummy, is *not* the novelist. The focus is on the time, the era, the historical circumstance, the society—not on Isherwood per se. Heilbrun quotes renowned short-story writer, novelist, biographer, and travel writer V. S. Pritchett on Isherwood: "'[Isherwood's] career represents the interaction of the reporter and the artist at its most delicate balance'" (*CI*, 16). Heilbrun spends several pages citing other critics as well on Isherwood's point of view, the reliability of his narrators, and his fictional technique (*CI*, 19). In the other novels—*All the Conspirators, The Memorial, The World in the Evening, A Single Man*, and *A Meeting by the River*—no ventriloquist's dummy appears. Heilbrun offers an analysis of all of these works.

She and other critics agree that of the documentary-style novels, the Berlin stories, including *The Last of Mr. Norris* and *Goodbye to Berlin*, catapulted Isherwood to fame. The characters are unforgettable and the voice unique to Isherwood. These novels show Berlin in its state of moral collapse and degradation as Hitler came to power. The character Norris emerges as a comic, miniaturized version of Hitler. Heilbrun notes that the Berlin stories introduced not only Isherwood's brilliant though cool evocation of Hitler's Germany but also that "ventriloquist's dummy 'Christopher Isherwood'" (*CI*, 5). *Goodbye to Berlin*, Heilbrun concludes, focuses on the theme of desertion and betrayal. "All of Isherwood's homosexual lovers," she writes, "are deserted by the boys they adore—it is as inevitable as aging. The exploitive, repetitive, constantly failing quality of these homosexual relationships seems to enlighten, in Isherwood's work, the futility of most passionate, driven attachments" (*CI*, 13). She maintains that the futility of these relationships is equated with "the destruction of hope, in the early books with Nazism and war, in the later books with the impermanence of love in modern society" (*CI*, 13).

Among the novels in which the dummy does not appear, Heilbrun and the critics she cites readily agree that *A Single Man* (1954) is the masterpiece, presenting a brilliant use of the theme of homosexuality. Like James Joyce's *Ulysses*, this novel spans the length of one day. A college professor, an expatriate Englishman who teaches English literature, has lost his male lover through death. Ironically, the novel is delightfully comic as George, the protagonist, goes to class, placates an alcoholic female friend, goes to a bar, talks with a highly intelligent student, and mocks American society and education. Heilbrun believes that "Point of view is the key to the novel's perfection" (*CI*, 43). Some may wish to read this novel simply for Heilbrun's statement that "[i]t contains the best American college classroom scene ever portrayed" (*CI*, 42). *A Single Man* from beginning to end is written in lyrical and seamless prose.

Although Heilbrun's essay is relatively brief, she covers Isherwood's biography, delineates his novels, and cites critical commentary on the books, concluding with Angus Wilson's comment that Isherwood was "close to the moral center of his generation" (*CI*, 46). This short book reflects Heilbrun's continuing interest in British subjects—from the Garnett family to Christopher Isherwood and on to her next publication, *Lady Ottoline's Album*.

Lady Ottoline's Album

To understand and sufficiently evaluate Carolyn Heilbrun's edition of *Lady Ottoline's Album*,[19] one will find Miranda Seymour's biography *Ottoline Morrell: Life on the Grand Scale* indispensable. A well-connected aristocrat, Lady Ottoline Violet Anne Bentinck (1873–1938) married Philip Morrell in 1902, and from 1907 until her death in 1938 she became the queen bee of London's literary society. She knew everyone of importance. Garsington Manor, her villa near Oxford University, became a magnetic field for people like T. S. Eliot, D. H. Lawrence, Virginia Woolf, Vanessa Bell, Bertrand Russell, Lytton Strachey, Katherine Mansfield, Augustus John, and dozens of other well-known writers.

Lady Ottoline became known for her generosity in providing lodging, food, and entertainment for these famous men and women, some of whom, like Strachey, casually accepted her hospitality and some of whom, like virtually all of the Bloomsbury group, incised her from the zyphoid to the pubis. She was envied and mocked for her supposed pretensions and, the "Bloomsberries" said, for her need to orchestrate. Still, as the Seymour biography makes clear, Lady Ottoline emerges as intelligent, perceptive, clever, generous, and forgiving. When offered proof concerning the blistering attacks against her by guests, especially by Lytton Strachey, she eventually forgave the aggressors.

Many, without any evidence, vilified her. David Garnett, who was invited by Lady Ottoline on the strength of his being the son of the famous translator, Constance, joined in the flailing of his hostess. His many negative comments about her in his autobiographical books were a combination of invention and hearsay. "Garnett's close friendship with both Strachey and Vanessa [Bell] provides the most plausible explanation for his later delight in guying Ottoline," writes Seymour. "To defend Ottoline was to risk being mocked with her" (Seymour, 207). People like

Virginia Woolf were jealous of Lady Ottoline's aristocratic background, her social connection, and her independent spirit.

Her friends and acquaintances in turn admired and deplored Lady Ottoline's flamboyant costumes. She enjoyed combining riotous colors, especially purple, crimson, yellow, orange, and red, and liked wearing high-heeled colorful shoes and enormous hats draped with gossamer and festooned with flowers.

Among her many admirers was Bertrand Russell, famous mathematician and philosopher, who fell madly in love with Lady Ottoline and wanted to marry her. Although Ottoline's marriage was not an especially happy one, she refused to leave Philip Morrell, known by his contemporaries as a philanderer. At one point in his life, two women, one a servant, were simultaneously expecting his children; two boys were subsequently born of these liaisons. Virginia Woolf dreaded and loathed being near him.

Traveling often throughout Europe and even to India, Lady Ottoline met virtually everyone of importance, including André Gide, eminent French novelist and philosopher, and the Russian ballet star Nijinsky. She generously patronized the arts and artists and contributed heavily to a shelter for prostitutes and indigent women. Always, she encouraged the young male students from Oxford to come to her teas and social activities to meet renowned people like William Butler Yeats, Thomas Hardy, and D. H. Lawrence.

Miranda Seymour alerts the reader that Michael Holroyd's *Lytton Strachey* (1968) presents a limited portrait of Ottoline Morrell as a "bizarre and untutored aristocrat . . . whose sole ambition was to gate crash her way into the secret world of the artist" (Seymour, 147). At the time of his research, Holroyd was not privy to Lady Ottoline's letters to Strachey. Reading Seymour's book gives one the impression that Ottoline Morrell in fact did not gate crash but actually provided the venue for artists, writers, and politicians to meet each other and to socialize with young men and women.

Some of the encomiums at Lady Ottoline's death reflect admiration, respect, and gratitude from many famous people. Virginia Woolf, who before Ottoline's death began to develop a close friendship with her, wrote that Morrell's death made her feel "rather lacerated . . . can't help feeling a queer loveliness departed" (Seymour, 398). T. S. Eliot's letter to Julian Morrell Vinogradoff, her daughter, expresses his grief at her mother's death: "I send you all my sympathy, dear Julian, but I haven't much to spare; I mean that my first feeling is of the loss to myself. . . . It is very difficult to think of things *without* anyone who meant so much to me" (Seymour, 416).

Along with hostessing, supporting worthy causes, and traveling, Lady Ottoline had an unusual hobby—photography. Her *Album,* edited by Heilbrun, contains snapshots and portraits of her eminent contemporaries, mostly literary, photographed mostly by Lady Ottoline; pictures of herself were taken by others, of course, especially by Baron de Meyer. The foreword to the *Album* by her daughter Julian Morrell Vinogradoff includes a number of pertinent details—that these photographs were taken by her mother (excepting those from circa 1902–10, taken by her father, Philip). Vinogradoff further relates that her mother used a variety of cameras, with the largest number of photographs taken with a Rolliflex. Using the best of German cameras, Lady Ottoline was a prodigal photographer, sending her films for development to the best of London's shops. Lady Ottoline's photographs were compiled in 12 albums. Her mother, says Vinogradoff, could always be seen with a camera before her left eye (*LOA,* 7).

Following the foreword is an introduction of 12 pages by Lord David Cecil, eminent historian, who as an Oxford student often visited Garsington Manor. Cecil discusses the *Album* as a pictorial record of Lady Ottoline "and the circle of which she was the center and creator. As such, it is a document of historic importance. For this circle was something unique in the social history of twentieth century England" (*LOA,* 3).

Cecil presents a brief biography of Lady Ottoline, followed by a list of 18 well-known figures in her circle—all friends, including Bertrand Russell, dear friend and lover. Cecil briefly reviews the pacifism of the Morrells during World War I, a distinctly unpopular and dangerous view to maintain. Lady Ottoline, six feet tall, is described by him as sensational, with rust-colored hair and a penchant for canary-colored silk and lavishly trimmed chapeaux. Garsington Manor, he declares, with its interior decoration, reflected the exquisite aesthetic taste of Lady Ottoline. This country seat became a magnet for bohemians like the artist Mark Gertler and the writer Siegfried Sassoon. Cecil then describes Ottoline as a lion, "a creative artist of the private life, whose imagination expressed itself in the clothes she wore, the rooms she sat in, the social life that took place there, and, more than anything in herself" (*LOA,* 10). Ottoline's interests extended even to a delight in fairs, music halls, and comedy; she entertained Charlie Chaplin with pleasure (*LOA,* 11).

Cecil met many literary men at Garsington and at Gower Street, London, a later Morrell residence. He relates a poignant episode wherein

Samuel Koteliansky ("Kot"), a Russian Jewish translator and friend of D. H. Lawrence, asked Lady Ottoline to invite T. S. Eliot so that he could berate the poet for turning to Christianity. He accused Eliot in person of turning to this religion from a cowardly desire for comfort. "Eliot rose to the occasion; his reply was deeply impressive. So far from Christianity being a comfort to him, he said, it was in some ways the reverse: for it had forced him to face the full dangers of the human predicament, not just in this life but for eternity; and it had burdened his soul with a terrible and hitherto unrealized weight of moral responsibility" (*LOA,* 13). Cecil says that "Kot" was silenced, and he himself felt that "he had been given a glimpse into the depths of Eliot's grand and tragic spirit" (*LOA,* 13). Ottoline was also moved; for the rest of her life she remained a confidante of Eliot, especially in the matter of Eliot's first wife, a victim of severe mental problems. Cecil's introduction strikes the reader as a tender, respectful, and fond tribute to Lady Ottoline.

Lady Ottoline's Album is a veritable visual panorama of literary and other celebrities—196 photographs in all. Carolyn Heilbrun's contribution as editor involves her selection of suitable excerpts from letters, diaries, poems, and other prose used by Lady Ottoline and the guests who flocked to her teas, dinners, and weekends at Garsington Manor and the two London residences at Bedford Square and Gower Street. These selections by Heilbrun complement the variety of photographs that constitute almost an embarrassment of riches.

Predominantly featured is Lady Ottoline as she appears in 47 photographs, the largest number in the *Album.* Although there is a particularly beautiful and regal photograph of her taken in a studio in 1912 and often reproduced in books about her, it is not included. There are, however, many others in the *Album* that reveal the peculiar attractiveness of this doyenne: she is photographed as a child, a debutante, on her Paris honeymoon, in Venice in a gondola, in St. Mark's Square feeding the pigeons, and at a hotel gondola esplanade wearing her enormous and flamboyant hats and her pearls. Although her Roman nose may seem protuberant to the casual viewer, this feature actually merges into a finely sculptured face with large expressive eyes. Dozens of writers called her beautiful. Always in these photographs she gazes with no self-consciousness. Ottoline is photographed with Lytton Strachey, Virginia Woolf, T. S. Eliot, and Mark Gertler, the painter. Carolyn Heilbrun selected this excerpt accompanying the honeymoon pictures from Ottoline's *Memoirs:* "I didn't really think of marrying then, and clung to my solitary liberty. I believe in many women there is a strong intuitive feeling of pride in their solitary life that when marriage really comes it is, to a certain extent, a humiliation" (*LOA, 20*).

A paragraph from D. H. Lawrence's *Women in Love* accompanies two facing pages of three head views of Lady Ottoline, who knew and resented Lawrence's use of her as a model for his Hermione Roddice, on the whole an unflattering portrait of Ottoline. This excerpt suggests ambiguity. "She was a woman of the new school, full of intellectuality and heavy, nerve-worn with consciousness."[20]

There are several photographs of Lady Ottoline swimming in Venice, wearing a huge veiled hat even in the lagoon. In the accompanying excerpt, taken from her *Memoirs,* she exclaims, "Italy has ever been in my imagination the land of my freedom. . . . As I look back on the years that followed and trace my wanderings, I see I was more in Italy than in England" (46–47). Accompanying a photo of Lady Ottoline opposite the Red Room and the Green Room at Garsington Manor, David Garnett is quoted from his book, *The Flowers of the Forest,* "She had transformed [the rooms], stamping her personality ruthlessly everywhere" (108–9).

Lytton Strachey, one of the frequent guests at Garsington Manor, appears in 15 photographs, bearded, bespectacled, thin, and short. Often he appears like a woeful, preaching Jeremiah. He poses with Virginia Woolf in other photos, unengaged with her. At other times, he stands alone or sits with William Butler Yeats. Carolyn Heilbrun selected several excerpts from Michael Holroyd's *Lytton Strachey* for the album. One relates Strachey's visiting Lady Ottoline, who describes him as arriving "an emotional, nervous and physical wreck, ill and bruised in spirit, haunted and shocked." Lady Ottoline writes that she offered Strachey a sitting room to write in "and he stayed some time."[21]

The third most predominant subject of *Lady Ottoline's Album* in frequency of appearance is that of Virginia Woolf of the Bloomsbury coterie. The writer of such classic novels as *Mrs. Dalloway* and *To the Lighthouse* and of the well-known feminist tracts *Three Guineas* and *A Room of One's Own* appears in 23 pictures. In the *Album* Woolf is portrayed on four successive pages smoking, sipping, reading, listening, and smiling. These may appear uncharacteristic moods to even the casual reader of any Virginia Woolf biography who knows the tortures of the mind experienced by her and which eventually led to a series of suicide attempts and the final successful suicide in 1941. William Plomer's *Recollections of Virginia Woolf* paints a brief but sharply etched portrait. "She liked good talk, good food . . . and good coffee. I see her in a shady hat and summer sleeves, moving by the fig tree and smoking one of her favorite cheroots; I see the nervous shoulders, the creative wrists, the unprecedented sculpture of the temples and eye-sockets; I see her grave and stately, or in a paroxysm of happy laughter."[22] In the *Album* photos, Woolf is seen relaxing with Lytton Strachey, chatting with Lord David Cecil or G. Lowes Dickinson, or standing alone, flirtatious or introspective, her statuesque, slim figure enveloped in a huge multicolored scarf. Heilbrun selected for a page of two full-length photos a quote from Woolf's *To the Lighthouse*. "'Was it wisdom? Was it knowledge? Was it, once more, the deceptiveness of beauty, so that all one's perceptions, halfway to truth, were tangled in a golden mesh? Or did she lock up within her some secret which certainly . . . people must have for the world to go on at all?'"[23] These lines characterize some of the elements of Woolf—intuitive person and gifted writer. In the *Album*, wherever Woolf appears, she is usually the cynosure of attention and attraction; at least she has been thus framed by the lens of Lady Ottoline.

Philip Morrell appears in 11 photographs—on his honeymoon in Paris, with his child Julian, with Bertrand Russell, Lytton Strachey, and Virginia Woolf. Only one photo of Lady Ottoline with her husband appears in the *Album*, a silent commentary, he looking at her and she gazing into the camera. Three pictures of Philip Morrell, on two facing pages, are accompanied by a passage from Trevor Wilson's *The Downfall of the Liberal Party* (1914–35), insofar as Philip had been a Liberal member of Parliament. "Liberals [said Philip Morrell] should not abandon in this conflict the principles of individual liberty—free trade, free service, freedom of opinion—which had made Britain one of the best-governed and most prosperous countries in the world."[24]

T. S. Eliot appears in seven photographs—smiling at Ottoline and Mark Gertler and visiting with undergraduates. Several pictures include Lord David Cecil, then a student. Quotations from T. S. Eliot's "Christianity and Communism" and his "East Coker" segment from *Four Quartets* may not particularly interest readers.

On one page there appear three photographs of André Gide, sophisticated and relaxed, with not a whit of self-consciousness before the camera. E. M. Forster's quote from his *Two Cheers for Democracy* is an apposite one: "[Gide] has taught thousands of people to mistrust facades, to call the bluff, to be brave without bounce and inconsistent without frivolity. He is the humanist of our age—not of other ages, but of this one."[25] A few pages following there is a full page of four photographs of Forster. He looks like T. S. Eliot's Prufrock, with his trousers appearing rolled up or talking with Mark Gertler or reading or just relaxing in a wicker chair in the Garsington Manor garden. A full-page quote from two sources accompanies the photos of Forster. One, P. N. Furbank's "The Personality of E. M. Forster," published in *Encounter*, includes the trenchant comment that "he knew how to live in daily touch with his own depths."[26]

Included among the many pictures of celebrities in literature and other fields are five extant exterior photographs of Garsington Manor, an attractive house of three stories with gables, a lake with statuary, interior views of the Green Room and the Red Room, revealing Oriental rugs, fireplaces, flowers, keepsakes, and comfortable furniture. Many of the guests commented on Lady Ottoline's combination of vibrant colors and her impeccable interior decorating. In Siegfried Sassoon's *Siegfried's Journey*, he agreed with others that the house was enchanting and called it "'an absolute dream of beauty.' It was surely no wonder that Lady Ottoline felt romantic and poetical in such surroundings."[27]

In the *Album* the photographs taken by Lady Ottoline and others, and the supplemental writings accompanying those photographs, coalesce into portraits frozen in time. They suggest nostalgia for the era between World War I and World War II, when the Bloomsbury group and others—witty, literate, productive, and eccentric—were invited to gather in an English manor house by Lady Ottoline. Some of the many facets of London's quintessential hostess in this time frame are captured in Virginia Woolf's obituary of Lady Ottoline. "With what imperious directness, like that of an artist intolerant of the conventional and the humdrum, [Ottoline] singled out the people she admired for qualities that she was often the first to detect and champion, and brought them together at Bedford Square and then at Garsington. . . . She created her own world" (*LOA*, 76).

Carolyn Heilbrun, then, in selecting extracts from an assortment of diaries, novels, letters, and poems, shows her familiarity with a wide range of Bloomsbury-era literature. For Heilbrun, this particular literary era will reappear in a variety of contexts in a number of books she will write on women, feminism, and literature.

Chapter Three
Early Feminist Writings

This chapter examines Carolyn Heilbrun's shift of focus from people in British literature to the subjects of gender and feminism—in the books *Toward a Recognition of Androgyny* (1973) and *Reinventing Womanhood* (1979). In *Toward a Recognition of Androgyny* Heilbrun traces what she believes to be a "hidden" river of androgyny in mythology and literature and explored her belief that a truly civilized society would reject rigidly defined roles based on gender. *Reinventing Womanhood* presents Heilbrun's thesis that women, long subject to a patriarchal definition of womanhood, must reinvent that definition for themselves so that it includes such qualities as independence, assertiveness, ambition, and achievement. In *Reinventing Womanhood* Heilbrun strikes one of main themes featured here in *Carolyn G. Heilbrun*—woman as outsider and reveals some of her personal history to exemplify her ideas.

Both *Toward a Recognition of Androgyny* and *Reinventing Womanhood* advocate the rejection of sex-based stereotypes and the encouragement of women's emotional independence; and in both Heilbrun turned to literature and history to present her convictions. The decade during which she worked on these books was an important one for her development as a scholar and a feminist. It is in the 1970s that Heilbrun became affiliated with a number of national literary organizations and centers for women's studies. While her long-time interest in modern British literature and biography would continue to inform her work from this period on, her interest in feminism would be more likely to direct it.

Toward a Recognition of Androgyny

Guiding Heilbrun's turn toward feminism with the publication of her fourth book, *Toward a Recognition of Androgyny,* were her perceptions of two kinds of oppression of women: that imposed by mainstream society and that imposed by themselves. In perceiving themselves as powerless, Heilbrun states, women make themselves so.

Part 1: "The Hidden River of Androgyny"   Heilbrun begins by reminding the reader that *androgyny* is a combination of two Greek words: *andro* (male) and *gyn* (female). *Androgyny,* she writes, defines "a condition under which the characteristics of the sexes, and the humane impulses expressed by men and women, are not rigidly assigned. Androgyny seeks to liberate the individual from the confines of the appropriate."[1] Heilbrun early cites her belief that our future salvation inheres in a direction away from "sexual polarization and the prison of gender toward a world in which individual roles and the modes of personal behavior can be freely chosen" (*TRA,* ix–x). Although she sees in the concept of androgyny the promise of reconciliation between men and women, she recognizes that it is nonetheless largely perceived as a threat. Any change threatening institutions and habits—no matter how ill advised—is also viewed as a menace to individual security. Androgyny, Heilbrun asserts, creates more fear in both men and women in the sexual than in the social sphere. If, as Heilbrun insists in her apologia for androgyny, there appears a plea for feminism, it results from the power held by men and the relative political weakness of women.

Throughout the book, Heilbrun's thesis reflects a strong, comfortable command of literature; she calls her tract an essay, with the first part a tracing of the hidden river of androgyny. Admitting a debt to Joseph Campbell, the renowned mythologist, and to his five-volume *The Masks of God: Occidental Mythology,* Heilbrun cites this work for its "extraordinary record of the ancient shift from matriarchy to patriarchy" (*TRA,* 5). Greece, Heilbrun argues, extolled women in pre-Periclean Athens by naming its main city after the goddess of wisdom. In Periclean times, women became submerged, but what she calls the "feminine" impulse (toward love and peace) as opposed to Joseph Campbell's idea of "masculine" impulse (force as a suitable expression) persisted in that the great tragedies reflected feminine virtues in many male characters (*TRA,* 4–5).

Using characters like Antigone and Teiresias from Greek tragedy, Heilbrun alludes to Ovid and T. S. Eliot in interpreting these figures to be androgynous. She then examines women in the time of Jesus, in the Middle Ages, and in the Renaissance, with particular emphasis on Shakespeare's plays. In all of the allusions to these plays, if men ignore the feminine impulse as they assert what is generally accepted as attributes of men, they lose much of their humanity. Church fathers are indicted for their fear of sexuality, a position that reinforced their fear of women. In focusing on the Shakespearean comedies of forgiveness, such as *The Winter's Tale,* Heilbrun portrays some heroines as possessing what she calls "the grace of androgyny" (*TRA,* 33), that capacity to make a better world. She concludes that Shakespeare in his last plays envisioned a redeemable world because of its androgyny, a fusion of the best impulses that both men and women possess. Shakespeare is androgynous.

Part 2: "The Woman as Hero"   In the first section of this second part of the book, Heilbrun primarily discusses English novels that embody the "feminine" impulse, that employ woman as hero. Heilbrun defines *hero* as the personification of an artistic vision by male writers; in the works of these writers, "a woman would bear the burden of the tragic action" (*TRA,* 49). Heilbrun cites 1880 as the year of invention of the woman as hero by Henrik Ibsen and Henry James, and for 50 years, other writers, such as George Bernard Shaw, D. H. Lawrence, and E. M. Forster, used women as their center of imagination. Heilbrun relies heavily on Ian Watt's *The Rise of the Novel*[2] and Agnus Wilson's *The World of Charles Dickens*[3] for many of her interpretations, including Dickens as nonandrogynous, even misogynistic. Heilbrun applauds Daniel Defoe in portraying Moll in *Moll Flanders* (1722) as androgynous, unencumbered by her sex.

Samuel Richardson, author of *Clarissa* (1747–48) and *Pamela* (1740), was quick to recognize a danger and a loss to society in denying women a place in the sun. Heilbrun dwells at length on Richardson's *Clarissa,* a novel of sexual polarization. Interestingly, when the novel first appeared, the scoundrel Lovelace, who drugs and then rapes Clarissa, invoked empathy in many readers, while today most critics see Clarissa as the victim of Lovelace's sexual rapacity. Heilbrun categorizes this novel as "the first cry of outrage against the almost total betrayal of the androgynous ideal" (*TRA,* 59). She joins many commentators who condemn Lovelace not only for the heinous rape but also for his total lack of identification with his victim and for his consideration of Clarissa as mere sexual baggage; he attains not a scintilla of spiritual awareness. Lovelace, says Heilbrun, having committed the despicable act of rape, "has betrayed himself into a sterile male universe" (*TRA,* 62–63), with no possibility of becoming conscious of any feminine impulse, a term that Heilbrun repeatedly employs. Her coda to the discussion of *Clarissa* is that "Lovelace forgets Clarissa is a human being and is doomed. The society which has failed to teach him her humanity stands also condemned" (*TRA,* 62). Clarissa's family, who would have had her marry another thoroughly unsuitable male, together with Lovelace, are metaphors for this doomed society, completely oblivious to the androgynous ideal.

In the second section of part 2 Heilbrun focuses on four great novelists of the nineteenth century—all of them women: Jane Austen, Emily and Charlotte Brontë, and George Eliot (Mary Ann Evans). "The force of the hidden androgynous impulse in the nineteenth century," Heilbrun writes, "is nowhere better demonstrated than in the stature of the major women novelists" (*TRA,* 73). These novelists use androgynous figures in portraying women Heilbrun calls heroes. Many readers know that the Brontës assumed names that suggested either sex; their novels were applauded generously only when male critics thought them to be written by men.

Despite some critics categorizing Jane Austen as feminist, Heilbrun discards the idea. Rather, she believes, Austen's brilliance lies in her artistic portraiture of a society in which men and women intermingle with equality. In Austen's universe, both genders assume moral and social responsibility for their behavior. This novelist's use of the "mores of her world to give a sense of the actual contribution of men and women to the moral atmosphere" (*TRA,* 75) fascinates Heilbrun.

Considering Austen a genius of absolute androgyny, Heilbrun discusses the parade of women heroes in her novels, especially Emma in *Emma* (1815) and Elizabeth Bennet in *Pride and Prejudice* (1813), women who do not need men for their self-identification and who hold their own in dialogues with men. Austen breathes similar life into the men she creates—men who recognize the feminine impulses within themselves—the Knightleys and the Darcys. Austen's carefully modulated laughter and irony, sparing neither man nor woman, validates a world in which the sexes need not engage in deadly combat. In *Pride and Prejudice* and in *Emma,* two of Austen's more important novels, the final pages end with gentle and satisfying rapprochement. Heilbrun has shown Austen to be in tune with the forces that bind the best in men and in women.

By contrast, Charlotte Brontë, author of *Jane Eyre* (1847) and *Villette* (1853), among other novels, from Heilbrun's stance, does not basically reflect an androgynous vision. *Villette* unfolds as the struggle of a woman in a world that fails to recognize talent and genius. In *Jane Eyre,* the most popular of Charlotte Brontë's books, Jane holds to her moral values, refusing to become Rochester's mistress, but the sexual magnetism limits the novel's range. According to Heilbrun, although Brontë exhibits a crystal-clear awareness of the insurmountable difficulties that gifted women face in determining their destiny, the androgynous ideal is never expressed, only implied. Heilbrun writes of Charlotte Brontë, "No woman writer struggled as she struggled against the judgments of sexual polarization, nor resented them so fervently, nor so vividly expressed the pain they cost" (*TRA*, 78). Yet, unlike Austen, whose artistic balance accommodates both men and women, Brontë's literary vision lacks an evident calibration for androgyny.

Emily Brontë, Charlotte's sister, who wrote the well-known *Wuthering Heights* (1847), looms like a planet for having designed this tragic novel that Heilbrun considers purely androgynous. "The sense of waste, of lost spiritual and sexual power, of equality of worth between the sexes, is presented with no specific cry for revolution, but with a sense of a world deformed" (*TRA*, 59). What could be more androgynous than Cathy's poignant cry, "I am Heathcliff!" Heilbrun's analysis of this novel within her theme is penetrating. Initially, Heilbrun writes, Catherine and Heathcliff's love symbolizes the unexpressed androgynous ideal. Subsequently they betray this ideal, he by leaving and she by marrying Linton. Cathy calls out, but Heathcliff does not hear her cry that "he's more myself than I am." Heilbrun believes that in marrying Linton Cathy submerged her masculine side. As she is dying, Cathy "has recognized that she will take Heathcliff with her into death because 'he's in my soul'" (*TRA*, 81). Heathcliff, asking the dying Cathy what kind of life she thinks he will lead when she dies, says, "'Oh, God! Would you like to live with your soul in the grave?'" (*TRA*, 81).

After Cathy's death, Heilbrun declares that Heathcliff follows the masculine pattern of "violence, brutality and the feverish acquisition of wealth" (*TRA*, 82), even as Catherine has trod the conventional road of her sex into passivity, weakness, and luxury. Both have sunk into the usual roles of their sex—and therein lies the tragedy.

The second generation of young Catherine and young Hareton will at last find a way to exchange their skills and perhaps begin to approach androgyny. Heathcliff dies, still suffused with grief and rage at the destiny that has destroyed him. Heilbrun ends the discussion of *Wuthering Heights* with a salient comment: "The miracle consists in [Emily Brontë's] ability imaginatively to recreate in art the androgynous ideal which she perceived within herself on the loneliness of the moors" (*TRA*, 82).

The last nineteenth-century woman novelist Heilbrun discusses in this section of part 2—George Eliot—receives her accolade for having a mind that is absolutely androgynous: "Perhaps no individual whose life has been passed in the cultural center of her time has so embodied the 'masculine' and 'feminine' impulses conjoined," Heilbrun writes (*TRA*, 82). Eliot possessed a strength of mind that some still consider masculine and a sensibility that some consider feminine. In her novels, George

Eliot presents women who face many constraints and have no outlet for their talents; thus no androgynous character is portrayed. Ironically in Eliot's life and personality, as Heilbrun reminds the reader, both masculine and feminine traits were accommodated.

In *Middlemarch* (1871–72), one of the great Eliot novels, both Dorothea Brooke and Lydgate err in their choices and judgments, especially in their selection of mates, and both are disappointed, frustrated, and disenchanted. Both are injured by the repercussions of marriage. Heilbrun believes that both commit errors typical of their sex: Dorothea downgrades herself by accepting the position of "Milton's daughter," a reference to being a handmaiden to a more important person. Lydgate permits himself to be swayed by the beauty and superficial charm of a woman who limits and narrows his destiny. Lydgate initially scoffs at Dorothea's moral sense, although he lacks this virtue himself, but recognizes Dorothea's capacity for friendship. Eventually, Lydgate perceives Dorothea's strength, although it is too late for him to benefit from a woman's puissance. Heilbrun writes, "The androgynous ideal is, in the world of George Eliot's realism, never allowed consummation" (*TRA,* 85). Ideally, Dorothea and Lydgate, had they married, might have worked toward the androgynous ideal.

In Eliot's last novel *Daniel Deronda* (1876), Heilbrun believes the androgynous theme has been abandoned. Daniel and Gwendolen Harleth's stories are not connected thematically, lacking the brilliance shown in *Middlemarch.* The female protagonist is left to an uncertain destiny and the male lead character is involved in religion, which since the Jewish tradition considers women clearly subordinate to men, compounds the irony. In this novel, no androgynous fusion occurs.

The third section of "The Woman as Hero," considered by Heilbrun to be the most important, discusses "the climactic period twenty years each side of the turn of the century in which the woman as hero played an absolutely central role in the world of male writers" (*TRA,* 51). Heilbrun begins by citing Anton Chekhov as the writer from this period who was "best attuned to the 'feminine' impulse and who understood the ways in which society frustrates it" (*TRA,* 87). Tolstoy, she asserts, failed completely to create fictional characters within the purview of androgyny; not even the well-known Anna Karenina qualifies. Dostoyevsky, however, in his depiction of vibrant women, created "reverberations we expect from the androgynous novel" (*TRA,* 89).

Heilbrun then discusses the work of Henry James and Henrik Ibsen, the renowned Norwegian playwright, in the context of the modern woman as hero. This kind of woman is different from the earlier characters who were central. Such a woman "conformed to the definition of a tragic hero, and she was exclusively the imaginative creation of male writers" (*TRA*, 91). Heilbrun believes that these authors had no urge to espouse feminism but found that the woman's position in the universe afforded a suitable metaphor for their literary interests. She quotes Ibsen, who said that he was not writing about women's rights: "I am writing about humanity."

Ibsen's *A Doll's House* (1879) receives particular scrutiny because of Nora, who at the end of the play decides to leave her husband and her children in an attempt to find her identity, apart from that of wife, mother, and housekeeper. Nora asserts some of the positive virtues of men in her refusal to continue being her husband's "doll" and in her decision to take action in the forging of her own destiny.

Next, Heilbrun discusses Henry James's *The Portrait of a Lady* (1881), wherein Isabelle Archer marries an Italian who is interested in her money. Because she has promised Pansy, her stepdaughter, to return, Isabelle will not abandon her failed marriage. Heilbrun cites Isabelle's statement, "I know that nothing else expresses me." In other words, no possession and no one else defines her. According to Heilbrun's analysis, "Here it is the woman who, through the vision of the androgynous artist"—that is, Henry James—"speaks for modern man" (*TRA*, 96). According to Leon Edel's biography of Henry James, Heilbrun says, James saw woman not as an "other" but as a vision of man's inner self. For Henry James, the woman became a hero.

Still another male writer discussed by Heilbrun, E. M. Forster, wrote a number of novels well known to readers of English literature. His first three examine the theme that "men and women share the moral burden of the search for a new sexual awareness" (*TRA*, 97). In *Howard's End* (1910), from Heilbrun's view, Forster portrays a woman hero especially in Margaret Schlegel, who with her sister, Helen, rejects society's definition of that which is "right" or "normal." Forster gives his women freedom from following the dictates of their culture in their attitudes or actions.

One of Forster's artistic interests is to give women, with their constricted lives, a new concept of identity. The hero Margaret says, "All over the world men and women are worrying because they cannot develop as they are supposed to develop." And here the issue of Forster's homosexuality comes into play, as Heilbrun addresses it to assess its possible impact on his portrayal of women. Since society's norms prohibited

Forster from depicting homosexual men (his novel *Maurice,* with its homosexual themes and characters, was published only posthumously in 1971), Heilbrun finds Forster's androgyny apparent in much of his fiction. In *A Passage to India* (1924), Heilbrun defines Adela Quested as hero because "she makes a fool of herself in the cause of justice" (*TRA,* 99), recanting her initial charge against Aziz. Neither beautiful nor charming, Quested is unconfined by traditional femininity, and Forster creates empathy for her. Because Forster had to submerge his atypical view of sexuality even in print, says Heilbrun, he managed to capture a rare essence of friendship as he created characters whose bonds often went beyond sexuality.

Heilbrun believes that "androgyny, or the recognition of the feminine principle is central . . . only to a society that does not consider women defined by their love of men and children; like men, they must live in a world of far-ranging choices" (*TRA,* 100). An overlooked aspect of Forster's novels, Heilbrun believes, is "the importance for personal salvation of the odd and momentary relationship, the flash of love between two people who are not joined according to any of the conventional unions sanctioned by society" (*TRA,* 100). Both Forster in his novels and George Bernard Shaw in his plays write of friendships—one of the least explored human experiences in literature—shadowed by carnal relationships. In *Howard's End* Margaret and Henry Wilcox learn something of the feminist spirit, claims Heilbrun, and she insists that the masculine and feminine spirits cannot remain apart without unhappy consequences.

The next major English novelist Heilbrun explores is D. H. Lawrence, whose concepts of women and sexuality are often diffuse and frequently anti-woman. Heilbrun asserts that *Lady Chatterley's Lover* (1954) demeans women, while *The Rainbow* (1915) presents the myth of the woman newly born into a universe that the masculine spirit has ruined. Lawrence employs three myths in the earlier novel: that of Noah, of Eve's creation, and of the ceremony of birth, that is, the rebirth of oneself in spiritually parenting another. In *The Rainbow,* says Heilbrun, each birth is of a female, whose recognition (of spiritual parenthood) by the "new" parent gives "birth" to a spiritual heir. When this third myth is worked out by Lawrence in the novel, Heilbrun continues, "It has culminated in the creation of Eve, which is a self-creation" (*TRA,* 103). "The new Eve creates herself only after experiencing all the possible ways in which a woman is supposed to be able to 'become oneself'" (*TRA,* 109). Once she fashions herself, she is alone. Lawrence uses the image of a kernel, free to take root and to sprout. Heilbrun admits her surprise that Lawrence was able to write this kind of novel.

The last woman as hero Heilbrun discusses in this context is Saint Joan in the play of the same name by George Bernard Shaw. Heilbrun writes, "Shaw's Saint Joan is an extraordinary creation largely because Shaw knows that Joan is not only a woman hero; she is the prototype of the woman hero" (*TRA*, 110). Even though Saint Joan had only the most circumscribed of lives, she refused to be passive and instead followed a course that revolutionized France and perhaps the world. "The cause, moreover, for which she chose death," writes Heilbrun, "was simply freedom—freedom to live as a functioning moral being in the world" (*TRA*, 111). Shaw portrays a "female being with masculine aptitudes who, in her sainthood, reminded humanity of the need for feminine impulses in the world. Joan is an androgynous figure" (*TRA*, 111).

In concluding her discussion of woman as hero, Heilbrun laments that post–World War II novelists like Malamud, Roth, Bellow, and Mailer not only do not write about the woman as hero but actually demean and exploit her. Heilbrun has in this part of the book supported her thesis well, although some readers might appreciate more detailed illustrations and analyses of some particulars of the literary works she has selected.

Part 3: "The Bloomsbury Group"   Opening part 3 of *Toward a Recognition of Androgyny* is a quote from Virginia Woolf: "'Everyone is partly their ancestors; just as everyone is partly man and partly woman'" (*TRA*, 115). Heilbrun will integrate the content of the quote into her text. Bloomsbury, argues Heilbrun, may not be the apotheosis of the androgynous spirit, but it is the first actual example of such a life in practice.

As Heilbrun reminds those who have some knowledge of the Bloomsbury coterie, they were considered waspish and cultist, but she hopes to present a view that will offer another reasonable critical position. She quotes Angus Wilson, British novelist and critic, who when young had attacked Virginia Woolf's work but who later, when more mature, said he would hesitate to do so again. Heilbrun then offers what some readers might consider a highly speculative defense of the group, citing envy as a reason for some of the condemnation they received. The Bloomsbury group was sui generis, she states, because its members published more works of importance than did other such coteries and because they were androgynous. They were the first to lead their lives as if passion and reason were of equal heft. Clive Bell's *Civilization* (1936) is quoted at length to prove that essential to civilization are the equality of the feminine and masculine impulses and the Athenian respect for passion and intellect.

Heilbrun lauds the Bloomsbury intimates for being a community integrated with society; the group's men and women sharpened their verbal and critical skills through one another and followed the Athenian ideal of civilization. They valued art, claims Heilbrun, as the pinnacle of civilization. In discussing their capacity for love and joy, she notes that jealousy and domination were virtually absent. Anyone reading Miranda Seymour's *Ottoline Morrell,* discussed earlier in connection with *Lady Ottoline's Album,* may wish to disagree on many issues with Heilbrun, especially concerning Lytton Strachey, a Bloomsburyite who revealed waspishness and hypocrisy in accepting Lady Ottoline's hospitality and then ridiculing her behind her back. Virginia Woolf, too, is well known for her briar of a tongue.

In this part of the book Heilbrun often loses the thread of her argument for androgyny, although her detours provide absorbing reading. It is well to remember that when quoting Michael Holroyd's biography of Lytton Strachey, Heilbrun did not have access to some of the material used by Seymour in her biography of Morrell.

As is well known, the Bloomsbury group opposed war and violence and rejected Victorian stereotypes that sharply divided the definitions of "masculine" and "feminine." They did espouse "remarkable openness before new concepts of life and art" (*TRA,* 126). Interestingly, Heilbrun writes that without the two daughters of Leslie Stephen (who became Virginia Woolf and Vanessa Bell), the Bloomsbury group would have been less successful in their effort to reject the conventions of gender-based behavior. She quotes Quentin Bell, Virginia Woolf's nephew, who said that never before had women been on so completely an equal footing with men.

The Bloomsbury group productivity is astonishing. Virginia Woolf, the genius of the clique, a brilliant raconteur, published nine novels and several books of essays; Lytton Strachey wrote several biographies; G. E. Moore, the Cambridge philosopher, wrote *Principia Ethica;* Leonard Woolf, Virginia's husband, was a social activist, editor, and writer, and with her founded Hogarth Press; Vanessa Bell and Duncan Grant were portraitists; John Maynard Keynes, the gifted economist, wrote several books; Roger Fry, an art critic, published several books on art and architecture; and Bertrand Russell, philosopher and mathematician, published extensively in several areas. Heilbrun writes of them all, "Their perception of the androgynous nature necessary to civilization was embodied in their work as well as in their lives" (*TRA*, 135).

Lytton Strachey occupies a number of Heilbrun's pages, since she seems to believe that his virtues outweighed his faults. She praises his *Eminent Victorians*, although finds his analysis of Florence Nightingale wanting in underestimating the limitations placed on Victorian women. He is particularly harsh on the nurse of the Crimea because she buried her sexual self. Heilbrun believes Strachey commits a number of errors in portraying this renowned nurse and admits that in comparison with the three other essays (on males), this one is flawed. Heilbrun laments his identification of forcefulness with sexual perversion.

Strachey's *Queen Victoria* (1921) is next analyzed by Heilbrun. This book depicts a passive and mediocre queen who is a detriment to her nation. Heilbrun quotes Strachey in *Queen Victoria*, "'It was her misfortune that the mental atmosphere which surrounded her during these years of adolescence was almost entirely feminine'" (*TRA*, 145). Encouraged to develop only the "feminine" virtues and not her intellect or the "masculine" virtues, Strachey argues, she made England suffer. Had Victoria and Albert ruled together, combining their resources, her reign might have been memorable, Heilbrun concludes.

Lytton Strachey also wrote a biography of the first Queen Elizabeth, England's monarch extraordinaire. Heilbrun draws attention to two important observations Strachey made of Elizabeth—that her greatness resulted from the combination of her "femininity" and her "masculine" intellect and also that Elizabeth separated, like a man, her job from her sexual predilections. Heilbrun concludes that Strachey's characterization of the Renaissance queen of England ably limned her androgyny and attributed to it the brilliance of Elizabeth's reign.

Heilbrun leaves her examination of the genius of the Bloomsbury Group—Virginia Woolf—for last. She pays tribute to Winifred Holtby's *Virginia Woolf*,[4] which she considers the best biography on Woolf written before 1960. Holtby recognized the androgyny implied in the great novels, but she believed that Woolf never ignored the crucial role of sexuality. Heilbrun cites the significance of Holtby as a critic of Virginia Woolf in these words: "[She] perceived Woolf's central vision as embodying less an inner tension between masculine and feminine inclinations than a search for a new synthesis and an opportunity for feminine expression" (*TRA*, 154). Heilbrun considers *To the Lighthouse* (1927) Virginia Woolf's best androgynous novel (*TRA*, 156).

Discussing *To the Lighthouse* at length, Heilbrun believes that Mr. and Mrs. Ramsay depict the "masculine" and "feminine" roles respectively, a condition creating sexual polarization. Mrs. Ramsay can easily be interpreted as a mother-goddess. Heilbrun believes, however, that after his wife's death, Mr. Ramsay "will be able to offer his children androgyny, will discover he did not need her devouring, speechless love to affirm his children's being" (*TRA,* 160). Heilbrun mentions that "Virginia Woolf in this book has, in a fashion, said 'I am Mr. Ramsay'" (*TRA,* 156).

It is significant that Lily Briscoe, the artist who does not have to marry and chooses not to, relies on herself to shape her identity. The novel's final passage reflects her androgynous vision: "Love has a thousand shapes. There might be lovers whose gift it was to choose out the elements of things and place them together and [give] them a wholeness not theirs in life" (*TRA,* 163). Lily's words suggest that the artist's imagination conceives a multiplicity of choices in life, love, and art. She sees how the sexual polarization between Mr. and Mrs. Ramsay in their traditional roles limits the nature of their relationship. As Carol Woodring writes in his monograph *Virginia Woolf,* "Artists are androgynous unifiers of what life divides between the sexes."[5] A true artist, Lily envisions lovers who create their own landscape by selecting "elements" neither male nor female but who harmoniously combine the best of both, a wholeness of concept if not of reality. Heilbrun's overall analysis of the novel clearly shows an androgynous Lily, created by the most influential Bloomsbury artist, who was herself androgynous.

Heilbrun concludes her discussion of Woolf with the novelist's *Mrs. Dalloway* (1925), in which all marriages are seen as life denying. Heilbrun then briefly comments on *Orlando* (1928), that Woolf novel wherein the title character is a male and then a female. The succession of genders widens the perception of Orlando and leads him/her to believe that no basic difference in the genders exists. Heilbrun's coda is that we do not know what love is, "nor do we know what androgyny is. Woolf writes of a signal, no noisier than a single leaf detaching itself from a plane tree, but a 'signal pointing to a force in things which one has overlooked'" (*TRA,* 167).

In her afterword to *Toward a Recognition of Androgyny* Heilbrun states her belief that contemporary novelists (those then writing in the 1960s and 1970s)—neither men nor women—were writing androgynous novels. But she remained confident that such works would be written soon.

Critical Reception   Although some critics gave *Toward a Recognition of Androgyny* limited praise, on balance the reviews were negative. Heilbrun's first book of literary criticism, with its theme of androgyny, elicited commentary from a number of reviewers.

The well-known novelist Joyce Carol Oates found the book to be "an interesting, lively and valuable general introduction to a new way of perceiving our Western cultural tradition."[6] She notes the "fantastic" amount of reading Heilbrun did, but finds the overall effect of the book to be sketchy. Oates asserts that the term "androgynous ideal" is never made clear; it could mean many things. Pleased that Heilbrun avoids the excesses of criticism against D. H. Lawrence and shows sympathy in her analysis of *The Rainbow*, Oates nonetheless contends that Heilbrun is biased against Lawrence in failing to recognize that *Women in Love* is exactly the androgynous-ideal novel she might have praised. Oates goes on to express her puzzlement over Heilbrun's neglect of some contemporary novels that support her thesis, books by John Fowles and Doris Lessing. Finally, Oates remarks, "Unfortunately, when sexual politics enter literary criticism and when unique works of art . . . are to be put on trial, ransacked for stray sentences that appear to be chauvinistic, it is easy to lose one's equilibrium" (7).

A decidedly negative commentary on Heilbrun's book, written by an anonymous reviewer, appeared in the *Yale Review*. "Unfortunately," says the writer, "Heilbrun's book is so poorly researched that it may disgrace the subject in the eyes of some serious scholars."[7] The reviewer finds her image of the hidden river of androgyny to be flawed, since she establishes no link between the androgyne in earlier and later literature. The writer further believes that the culture's perception of the androgyne has changed over time. And Heilbrun is again faulted for her definition of androgyny, which is here labeled "idiosyncratic" and therefore of virtually no value. "Her terminology shifts fuzzily from page to page: sometimes androgyny is 'the equality of the masculine and feminine impulses'; more often it is 'the recognition of the feminine principle as central'" (viii).

This reviewer also discounts Heilbrun's views because she invests the androgyne with only positive qualities, while overlooking the dark, dangerous, and diabolical forces associated with the history of androgynes as they appear in the Roman Empire or the late nineteenth century. These allusions, the writer argues, are neglected because they would add fuel to the conventional belief that sexual fusion is "neurotic." Likewise, because Heilbrun's thematic development focuses on only a single category of androgyne, it is too narrow, says the reviewer, who states that there are at least 10 categories. The writer concludes his review with the following remarks:

> [Heilbrun] shrinks from pushing her theory to its necessary conclusion: surely if men may elect passivity, women may elect bloody-mindedness. But this is a book with a muddled, naively sentimental view of human nature: for Heilbrun "the hideous strictures" of society keep us from doing our own thing. There is not the slightest consideration of the rival claims of order, stability, and social coherence; no sense that multiplicity of role might be anarchic; no allusion to aggression or to the hormonal basis of behavior. . . . Everywhere, her error lies in making facile projections into actual life of a symbol that is principally an imaginative construction. (x)

Despite the faults found by critics, *Toward a Recognition of Androgyny* did succeed in introducing a number of stimulating books to some readers, while for more sophisticated readers it presented perhaps familiar books through a new lens—androgyny—and so made possible new perceptions. In the final analysis, the book's thematic recapitulation may be a challenge to men, women, and "androgynes."

Reinventing Womanhood

In *Reinventing Womanhood,* published in 1979 when she was 50 years old, Carolyn Heilbrun leaves her study of literature through the prism of androgyny to pursue her thesis that women, in being perceived by neither others nor themselves as powerful or independent, have thereby forfeited the opportunity to be powerful or independent. Women, she states, need to develop the recognition, the desire, and the courage to heighten and change their consciousness. Heilbrun, in fact, argues that there must be a reinvention of womanhood, one excluding the need for validation from men.

In the first chapter of *Reinventing Womanhood,* "Personal and Prefatory," Heilbrun takes what is for her the unusual step of talking about her own life. Responding to a request from me while researching this volume to learn some personal details of her life not available in any consulted source, she wrote in a letter dated 9 July 1994: "I have a deep disinclination to talk about myself, and am indeed notorious for disliking direct questions. . . . Indeed, the degree to which I wrote about myself in *Reinventing Womanhood* was one of the bravest acts of my life, undertaken because I then felt that the impersonal, high moral tone of most literary criticism was not appropriate or useful to women critics and essayists at that time."

In this first chapter of *Reinventing Womanhood* then, she relates certain facts of her life—as a child, as a student at Wellesley, as a teacher and professor at Columbia University (much of which was used as the source of biographical information in the first chapter of this volume)—as a kind of example to the woman reader. Heilbrun owes to her impersonality and separateness her ability to survive at Wellesley, where she claims she encountered anti-Semitism, and at Columbia University, where in the Department of English and Comparative Literature, she writes, her mettle was sorely tested because of gender. During her entire tenure at Columbia University—more than three decades—more men than women taught in the department. Claiming that she never denied being a Jew or a self-defined woman, she writes, "What I denied was the power they had to limit my *self*-development, to force me humbly rather than arrogantly, to suffer!" (*RW,* 22).

Of particular importance to Heilbrun was the grant she received from Radcliffe College's Institute for Independent Study in 1976–77. She reveled in the ideal working conditions, being a part of a community with other professional women and being given the opportunity to learn from experts in many disciplines, psychology included. These experiences took shape and would be articulated in her later writings, both in essays and tracts and in the Amanda Cross detective stories.

In this first chapter of *Reinventing Womanhood,* Heilbrun begins to formulate her conviction that women must constantly examine themselves and their society if they are to determine why the feminist movement advances a few steps and then retreats, how tokenism impedes progress and contributes to the bonding of successful women with men. Women have failed to become autonomous.

Carolyn Heilbrun strikes her theme almost at the end of the first chapter in writing, "Womanhood must be reinvented" (*RW,* 29). Women have largely been content to accept as a given dependency as a condition of their sex, she writes. Most of those women who have succeeded in the professions, in business, or in the arts have succeeded only as honorary men, neither bonding with women nor helping them but retaining their conventional femininity and sacrificing womanhood. She excludes from this group those women who have themselves gained from the women's movement and who have contributed to the advance of other women.

Some women, claims Heilbrun, like herself, moved against the current of the tide; some circumstance in their lives "insulated them from society's expectations and gave them a source of energy, even a sense of destiny, which would not permit them to accept the conventional female role. Some condition of being an outsider gave them the courage to be themselves" (*RW,* 30). It is somewhat apparent that Heilbrun is alluding to educated women, to affluent women, to elitist women, but she does not limit her argument to the privileged.

Although Heilbrun deprecates successful women who have become, in effect, honorary men, she recognizes the contradiction of her argument when she encourages them, as she writes, "I want to tell women that the male role model for autonomy and achievement is, indeed, the one they must still follow" (*RW,* 31). In pursuing her argument, Heilbrun insists that the family is a crucial entity wherein women traditionally were and primarily are today the nurturers. Now, both women and men must share the parenting. She believes that definitions of manhood and womanhood will change and that each sex will gain by abandoning Procrustean negative definitions of the other. Since historically men have dominated human experience, especially in defining womanhood, now womanhood can become that which is designed by women, not by men.

In the closing of this first chapter, Heilbrun, deeply involved in literature since her adolescence, designs a key role for literature, since it is both fruit of and nourishment to the imagination. She refuses to separate literature from life in her crusade to reinvent womanhood because in literature female despair and life's possibilities have been articulated. Although Heilbrun does not specifically state that imagination is the matrix, it seems evident that imagination is quintessential in creating and interpreting literature *and* in growing limitless possibilities of regeneration in women's lives.

"Woman as Outsider," chapter 2, presents an overview of the many ways in which women have been excluded from positions of power. Some sects in Judaism, for example, make women outsiders by limiting their participation in religious observations. Social and psychological pressures block women's ability to bond, since such subgroups would undermine male power.

Virginia Woolf, says Heilbrun, urged women first to recognize themselves as outsiders and then to try to eliminate their subservience. In *Three Guineas* (1938) Woolf proposed forming a Society for Outsiders that would support anti-war policies and remuneration for all women for their work, inside and outside the home (*RW,* 39).

A subtheme of woman as outsider is Heilbrun's discussion of the three stages of suffering identified in *Suffering* (1975) by Dorothee Soelle, the German theologian and writer. The first stage is mute suffering, which encourages powerlessness and submissiveness, a phase that Heilbrun believes most women in the world experience. The next stage is that of articulation, reached by a limited number of women in highly industrialized countries, and it results in the breakup of isolation, particularly during periods of active feminism when consciousness raising is likely to occur. Finally, the third level takes place when women accomplish change during a period of high feminism, when sufferers develop solidarity, agree on common objectives, and organize to reach other women by breaking the stranglehold of passivity and powerlessness.

Heilbrun is quick to note that Soelle does not apply her theory only to women; it is Heilbrun who feels the matrix is particularly germane to the condition of women. "Unlike other slaves and oppressed people," she writes, "women have rarely, in Western countries, been in the desperate position of having nothing to lose. . . . Women have tended not to recognize the pain inherent in lack of selfhood, or if they recognize it to the extent of responding with general depression and despair, they have been unable to articulate it" (*RW,* 67). Since Soelle's second stage of suffering is crucial, it is disappointing that women have failed to articulate their pain, except during active times of feminism. Even then, some women oppose such articulation.

During 1965–75, with the women's movement at its height, some women worked to block its advance, primarily to avoid pain, Heilbrun believes. In the end, if there is no articulation, depression is often the result of powerlessness and stasis.

Heilbrun's chapter 3, "Women Writers and Female Characters: The Failure of Imagination," develops the premise that women writers, who have themselves developed a realization of the self, show a failure of imagination when it comes to creating autonomous female characters. "Jane Austen cannot allow her heroines her own unmarried, highly accomplished destiny," writes Heilbrun (*RW,* 72). Male writers, however, including Thackeray, D. H. Lawrence, and Henry James, have succeeded in creating fictive women of autonomy.

In presenting her illustrations of successful women writers who fail to create women like themselves, Heilbrun cites Mary Renault. Some critics might question her disproportionate use of 13 novels by Renault, a highly successful author, who in her novels designs female stereotypes of dependence, subservience, and passivity while idealizing male heroes for their aggressiveness in war, their domination of and cruelty to women. Heilbrun asserts, "Renault finds it easy to agree with Plato in his epigraph to Dion, that all women are 'spun into the dark web on the day of their birth'" (RW, 79). Renault in her life reached an autonomy and freedom that she does not confer on her heroines. Other women writers, too, reveal in their fiction this failure of the imagination to depict women aware of their worth, among them Willa Cather, Edith Wharton, and the cerebral English writer Iris Murdoch. Although Willa Cather fashioned an independent woman as protagonist in *My Antonia,* the narrator is male. And Antonia experiences triumph as mother of sons. Murdoch had by 1976 written 18 novels; of those five were told in the first person—a male.

There are exceptions to the failure of women writers to create women of autonomy, notably Charlotte Brontë in having designed the fictional heroine Lucy Snow in *Villette.* Departing from fiction writers, Heilbrun indicts Hannah Arendt, who in *Thinking* scorned feminism and the quality of women's thought without acknowledging that imposition of sex roles in society militates against training women to think. Arendt, concludes Heilbrun, adopted the male perspective.

Two writers lauded by Heilbrun for using the imagination successfully are Gail Godwin, the American novelist and Adrienne Rich, the poet. "But until the years of the recent feminist movement," writes Heilbrun, "to tell the story, to continue the quest, to follow through the plot of accomplishment in an extended work of fiction has been all but impossible for women writers" (RW, 92).

"Searching for a Model: Female Childhood," chapter 4, leads Heilbrun to examine and reject the Freudian view that women's sex determines the development of their personality development. Both women and men can achieve hegemony through the Oedipal process. Like many feminists, Heilbrun rejects the Freudian belief that women envy the male's genitalia; women, in fact, yearn for the possession of male destiny. Adopting the model of male achievement by women posits men's responsibility in nurturing children and a restructuring of the family. A new model of behavior by women is a clear requisite for full equality.

Heilbrun echoes the belief of many women and some men when she quotes from Roy Shafer's article "Problems in Freud's Psychology of Women": "'Freud's estimates of women's morality and objectivity are logically conventional patriarchal values and judgments that have been misconstrued as being disinterested, culture-free scientific observations'" (RW, 100). She pays homage, however, to Freud's magnificent discovery in recognizing the process of stages in the development of children reaching the Oedipal phase, undergoing and surviving tensions within themselves, in their relationship with parents, and in society as a whole. Nonetheless, she faults Freud with this declaration, "The terrible, and terribly different burdens he cast upon males and females, however, evolved from an inevitably male-centered view of the human condition" (*RW,* 102–3).

Concerning female identification, Heilbrun recounts four discoveries: the basic sex is female, insofar as a fetus begins as female; core gender identity is assigned, not biological; the male child, not the female, has the most difficult maturation adjustment; the male's problem in shifting gender identification is made only with difficulty. Males who continue to identify with their mothers face severe sexual dysfunctions. Young females, on the other hand, need not shift identification away from their mothers and thus have fewer difficulties in this sphere.

Achieving identity for women, which is essentially developing autonomy, will be difficult in a society dominated by male power structures. Despite this obstacle, some women have nevertheless succeeded, and Heilbrun asserts the need to probe family history in determining patterns contributing to the resulting autonomy. Several circumstances producing achieving women are catalogued by Heilbrun—socializing forces, often of a foreign culture; birth position in a sibling structure, usually an only child or a firstborn or one with siblings much older or younger; an environment of all girls, either at home or in schools or colleges; a daughter who is virtually a son to a father serving as a strong and positive model; recognition of the mother's limitations in a society and vowing to avoid her fate. Heilbrun cites women whose profiles fall within these parameters: Helen Deutsch, Polish psychoanalyst; Cheryl Crawford, American theatrical producer, Russian-born Golda Meir, prime minister of Israel, 1969–74; Indira Gandhi, prime minister of India; Simone de Beauvoir, French intellectual, philosopher, and novelist; American Frances Perkins, first woman to serve in the U.S. cabinet.

Women have been preponderantly passive, a circumstance that arrests their development. "From fairy tales onwards, women's fantasies have been of themselves as the sleeping figure a man will awaken," writes Heilbrun (*RW,* 124). Women need to create their own destinies, to become protagonists and yet consider "men as models for human action, and say: that action includes me" (*RW,* 124). She urges women not to wait at home like Penelope but to venture out like her husband, Ulysses, to be active in creating their own destiny.

In chapter 5, "Search for a Model: History and Literature," Carolyn Heilbrun discusses what good women can derive for themselves from traditional male models in mythology and literature and how they must at the same time generate their own female models. To make her points, Heilbrun goes back into history and the early literature of the Greeks.

In the first 12 pages she focuses on her one-time professor and later colleague Lionel Trilling and his several books on culture, the self, the liberal imagination, sincerity, and authenticity. (Many of Heilbrun's views on Trilling are presented in the first chapter of this volume.) She makes a particularly cogent case that Trilling, a highly respected critic, in no way recognized the subordinate role of women and their quest for equality, either in his life or in his literary criticism. "He understood that what he called the 'bitter line of hostility to civilization' runs through modern literature, but he was constitutionally incapable of perceiving the source of that hostility: the revolution of the feminine in life" (*RW,* 125).

Trilling believed, writes Heilbrun, that "Women were beyond the consideration in his general statements about moral ideas, except insofar as they impinged upon the lives of men" (*RW,* 128). Men for Trilling were visualized as "encompassing, in all their actions, the moral condition of society" (*RW,* 128). Heilbrun states clearly that Trilling never referred to the feminine revolution without disparagement.

Heilbrun at length discusses Trilling's concept of literature, especially of the "self" in relation to "culture," but he "never really conceived the self as properly having its being within a female" (*RW,* 131). Trilling said that Freud warned women not to block men in their cultural responsibilities and not to insist that men use their energies for love and for family at the expense of their activities in the world. Heilbrun laments that this view virtually excludes women from "free activity," even from civilization itself. "When Trilling spoke of men, he meant not humanity, but males. He was adamant in his exclusion of women, from his theories" (*RW,* 132). Despite such exclusion, Heilbrun believes that if women read Trilling, they will gain by increasing their awareness of the "strength and fears of the civilization they must both infiltrate and overthrow" (*RW,* 132). Heilbrun readily acknowledges how much she herself learned about the interpretation of literature from Trilling.

Perhaps the underlying motif not expressed by Heilbrun is that Trilling's concept of civilization, culture, and literature is flawed by its narrowness in this virtual exclusion of one half of the human race. Heilbrun reminds readers who know of Trilling's admiration for Jane

Austen, the only female author he respected, that he often misunderstood her, especially in his belief that Austen did not conclude that woman is a moral force. Women reading Trilling's books on culture or literary interpretation and looking "for insights into life and culture must avoid any specific comments of his on women as women, and listen to the advice he gives" to young men (*RW*, 136). These women must specifically be aware of Trilling's narrations of the "quests and dreams and desires of young men in search of a self. It is in their accounts that a woman will learn most of what she needs to know about the search for sincerity" (*RW*, 136).

Heilbrun closes this discussion with a clear and definitive statement: "There can be no question that women's almost total lack of followers—of those who carry on, in an unbroken line, the work of achievement—has been the greatest deprivation in women's history" (*RW*, 137). The challenge for women, according to Heilbrun, is to both retain the image of the male model and to change it. She ultimately concludes, however, that no *male* models actually exist, only models of selfhood, through which women can learn to become active, independent, and adventurous participants in their own lives rather than passive and acquiescent observers.

In this chapter Heilbrun also probes the interpretation of the Eros and Psyche legend from several perspectives, namely that of Erich Neumann, who is more sensitive to women, and Jean Hagstrum, who is not. Heilbrun then evaluates fairy tales, including Cinderella and several Grimm fairy tales, and integrates into her argument *The Uses of Enchantment* by educator and psychologist Bruno Bettelheim, who in his narratives makes male use of female figures.[8]

In shifting focus to Greek and Shakespearean tragedies, Heilbrun urges women to project themselves into male roles, say into a Hamlet instead of an Ophelia, to begin discarding the limits of acceptable behavior imposed on them. Heilbrun builds a tantalizing frame of femininity through which to view some Greek plays, notably the figure of Clytemnestra in the *Agamemnon,* who is often judged to be masculine by unthinking critics. Even feminists would object to a mother's murder, no matter the symbolism, as the nadir of men's actions, but Heilbrun insists the death of Clytemnestra is not that of a woman but of motherhood, that brand which symbolizes its damaging qualities. "That principle, not its action in loving parenthood, but its establishment as an institution," Heilbrun writes, "must be demythologized and ritually destroyed" (*RW*, 154). Orestes and Electra, having murdered Clytemnestra, their mother, may now have power to develop their individuality and selfhood. The mother herself, in thrall to society's expectations of her and her lack of freedom, had abused her children, who rose to destroy her domination. As symbolism, the chain of events threatens neither the family nor society. What is at issue is not matricide but the death of motherhood, which Heilbrun calls an institution.

In the remaining pages of this chapter, Heilbrun writes a polemic against male imperialism in appropriating muses for their own use and urges women novelists onward, to do as women poets have done, to articulate "their anger at the world and their imagination of female authority" (*RW,* 169). Since poetry, as Adrienne Rich avows, is "'much more rooted in the unconscious, it presses too close against the barriers of repression'" (*RW,* 169) and is more likely to spill out. Heilbrun, however, places her hope in women novelists, believing they will go beyond the brink of selfhood, and quotes Adrienne Rich to support her view: "'No one has imagined us'" (*RW,* 170).

The penultimate chapter 6 of *Reinventing Womanhood,* entitled "Marriage and Family," presents a variety of attitudes in life and in fiction through the lens of reinventing womanhood. In much of English and American fiction, as in life itself, marriage is the triumphant and indispensable crowning event of women's lives, especially for those women petrified of spinsterhood and powerless in a society that grants its seal of approval to motherhood and the effacement of self.

Heilbrun marshals a number of contemporary novels by women to press her argument beyond Austen's famous rejoinder, "Reader, I married him." Despite the failure of marriage in England, women writers generally refused to acknowledge or to probe the consequences of a disastrous connubiality until George Eliot did so in her novels of the nineteenth century, especially *Middlemarch,* in which the author portrays several failed marriages. Her heroine, Dorothea Brooke, trapped in an abysmal marriage, is freed only upon the death of her husband Casaubon.

Male writers, too, failed to write about the claustrophobic effects of marriage on women. "American male novelists have always been notoriously uninterested in female destiny" (*RW,* 175), Heilbrun says. Henry James was an exception, but he is often classified as a virtual exile. James Dickey, the American novelist and poet, the historian Christopher Lasch, and Lionel Trilling, too, are marked as conservatives, yearning for the past when women were willing to remain at home and shore up men's egos.

Married women in fact and in fiction have longed for space of their own, most notably Virginia Woolf in *A Room of One's Own,* Doris Lessing in her well-known short story "To Room 19," and Barbara Raskin in *Loose Ends*—all yearning for respite from children, husbands, and domestic duties, desperately in need of a sanctuary, an environment in which to be themselves, not wife, mother, housekeeper. In marriage, even women like Sylvia Plath became acolytes to their husbands, seeming to revel in their having been published first and fearing to break the "fragile" male ego.

Marriage, claims Heilbrun, failing as it has been, can be preserved only with the restructuring of the family, with parenting to be done by both genders. "In insisting upon 'mothering' as the function only of one female figure, we have made impossible the companionship of men and women" (*RW,* 189). Heilbrun relies extensively on Nancy Chodorow's *The Reproduction of Mothering: Psychoanalysis and the Sociology of Gender.*[9] She urges women to examine new theories, among them one that "Chodorow and others have proposed in the interpretation of the Oedipus complex, that classic theoretical construct that relates personality development to family structure" (*RW,* 191). Freud's limitation of the Oedipus complex to males, say women writers, can be broadened to include all children. Present family structures encourage a cycle that produces girls impelled to mother and boys impelled to sally forth into the world, without a concept of parenting. Males, reared only by women, find separation from mothers as the sine qua non of maleness. Heilbrun believes this contributes to boys' developing rigid boundaries of ego and a sense of self but limits their ability to sustain relationships. "Men," asserts Heilbrun, "define themselves by their separation from women; women define themselves by their lack of separation, of selfhood" (*RW,* 193).

If men and women share parenting, "Neither boys nor girls will then identify separation as separation from the mother, nor conceive of the only alternative to her and her all-encompassing love as inevitably male" (*RW,* 193). Heilbrun strikes a modern note, despite the book's publication in 1979, in her pronouncement: "That children should arrive in the world, unwelcome and unprepared for, as the consequence of lust or sexual pleasure, is no longer supportable as an ideal except by the most retrograde theories of human behavior" (*RW,* 195). Once childbirth is seen as commitment by two people, the benefits will lead to the "symmetrical family," with men the beneficiaries of nurturance and intimacy. "From birth onward," writes Heilbrun, "the child must be held in its father's arms, no less than in its mother's, and experience male love" (*RW,* 195).

Heilbrun claims for women the control of their bodies to procreate or not and for men the right of their fatherhood. She sums up her argument in these words: "The sexual division of labor, Chodorow tells us, produces male dominance. And male dominance produces men incapable of living, and women incapable of selfhood. From this division we must turn" (*RW,* 196).

"The Claims of Woman," the last chapter of *Reinventing Womanhood,* primarily discusses power that men have and women lack. Heilbrun again inveighs against her male colleagues at Columbia, who in publishing a Festschrift, a collection of essays honoring Lionel Trilling, in 1977 perpetuated his lack of concern about women's inequality, his view of women's rights as merely a nineteenth-century social issue. Heilbrun attacks Daniel Bell, one of the contributors to the Festschrift, who echoes Trilling's ideas that there is a need to move beyond narcissism and egocentrism (concern for self) to a concern for community. She counters his argument by declaring that men do not need to construct selfhood; all aspects of their lives have built it for them. "Women, meanwhile," writes Heilbrun, "have played for men the nurturer and partaker of meekness: they have been willing, not to inherit the earth, but to wait patiently to inherit it from those who will honor their achieved meekness" (*RW,* 202). Women, insists Heilbrun, must construct a selfhood despite opposition from those in power, used to protect the privileges of men.

Reinventing Womanhood concludes on a sober, meditative, and cautious but hopeful note. "The past is male. But it is all the past we have. We must use it, in order that the future will speak of womanhood, a condition full of risk, and variety, and discovery: in short, human" (*RW,* 212).

This manifesto, the fifth nonfiction book by Carolyn Heilbrun, ignited the interest of a number of reviewers in newspapers and journals. Anne Hulbert in the *New Republic* wrote, "The book she emerges with is frustratingly uneven but thought-provoking."[10] Hulbert further believes that Heilbrun's book is overly polemical and prescriptive but ends her review with mixed praise, "Though her arguments tend to be loose and her emphases skewed, Heilbrun sets an inspiring goal: autonomy for the self and imaginative sympathy for a community—of women" (40).

Another reviewer, Margot Jefferson, writing in the *New York Times Book Review,* objects to Heilbrun's chastising of women novelists for not creating autonomous women characters, "while ignoring Colette,

Dorothy Richardson, Virginia Woolf, Christina Stead, and Doris Lessing, among others. . . . George Eliot, the Brontës, and Jane Austen are accused of having written novels to avoid confronting this sense [of themselves]. No, Professor Heilbrun does not reinvent; she falsifies and reduces."[11]

Still another critic, Sara Ruddick, a feminist and a faculty member at the New School for Social Research, presents a succinct overview of *Reinventing Womanhood,* but cautions the reader: "Summarizing Heilbrun's arguments does not do justice to her wide-ranging literary erudition, to the wit of her examples, or to her compelling personal style."[12] She agrees with many of her ideas, but writes, "Heilbrun tends to undervalue women's past and present endeavors. At the same time, she accepts too uncritically concepts of achievement and adventure which are both male and privileged" (551). Commenting on Heilbrun's belief that many problems in marriage would be minimized or solved by sharing parenting and couples' having dual careers, Ruddick feels that "These rational, just arrangements barely touch the conflict and alienation between men and women wrought by their long-standing differences in power, sensibility, and moral outlook" (552).

Finally, Ruddick compliments the book for its openness and generosity, inviting disagreement and assent, too. "*Reinventing Womanhood* is a challenging gift: Heilbrun's questions are central, her answers sensitive and intelligent. She writes out of a commitment to *women* with a compassion and courage we would do well to emulate" (553).

Chapter Four

The First Five Amanda Cross Mystery Novels

"Order threatened; order restored"

Like a Pallas Athena, who sprang fully formed from the head of Zeus, Amanda Cross, alter ego of Carolyn Heilbrun, leaped into life when her first detective novel, *In the Last Analysis,* was published in 1964. Heilbrun's smokescreen lasted six years, until an energetic scholar searched the copyright records.

Why did Carolyn Heilbrun wish or need to adopt a pseudonym for her detective novels? In *Writing a Woman's Life* she devotes chapter 6 to her adventures as a writer of mysteries and explains some of the reasons for her nom de plume. Most important, Heilbrun writes, is that she feared denial of tenure by Columbia University if she did not shield her identity. The writing of detective novels by scholars would be considered frivolous.

Another reason Heilbrun decided on a pseudonym was to free herself from the confines of her personal identity. In the nineteenth century, women writers like George Sand, George Eliot, and Charlotte Brontë all used aliases. These male pseudonyms gave them freedom to explore in their writing parts of life then thought inappropriate for consideration by the female mind. As Heilbrun says in *Writing a Woman's Life,* it also allowed them to create women characters "who might openly enact the dangerous adventures of a woman's life, unconstrained by female propriety" (*WWL,* 112). In 1963, when in her late 30s, Carolyn Heilbrun claimed that she, too, fervently yearned to create her own psychic space, another identity and role. "I sought to create an individual whose destiny offered more possibility than I could comfortably imagine for myself" (*WWL,* 114). Heilbrun mused over creating a male protagonist/sleuth but decided that, knowing little about men's thought processes, she would be better off with Kate Fansler: unmarried, fiercely independent, impervious to the opinions of others, affluent, attractive, brainy—and an academic.

Many readers of the Amanda Cross novels ask Heilbrun how she selected her pseudonym. She explains that she and her husband, James, stranded once in Nova Scotia, noted a nearby road sign, "MacCharles Cross." Her husband felt that should she need a pen name, this sounded suitable. Heilbrun selected "Cross" and then chose "Amanda" because the name seemed to have gone out of popular use.

Heilbrun enjoyed her secret identity. "Secrecy is power," she writes. "Secrecy gave me a control over my destiny that nothing else in my life, in those pre-tenure, pre-women's movement days, afforded" (*WWL,* 116–17). As she developed the character of Kate Fansler, Heilbrun was in a sense also re-creating herself, as women writers often do. Writing fiction permits Heilbrun "to write my own life on a level far below consciousness, making it possible for me to experience what I would not have had the courage to undertake in full awareness" (*WWL,* 120).

Alluding to both of her names, one real, the other fiction, Heilbrun writes, "Something happened to both Carolyn and Amanda: the women's movement" (*WWL,* 121). And in fact as Amanda Cross she weaves into her plot, dialogue, and action the themes of feminism and androgyny that are of such concern to Professor Heilbrun. As James Hillman writes in *Revisioning Psychology,* "An author's fictions are often more significant than his own reality, containing more psychic substance, which lasts long after their 'creator' has gone. An author creates only by their own authority."[1]

The genre of the detective story particularly appealed to Heilbrun by virtue of its mystery and the consequent disarray, the momentum given by plot, characters, and action until the moment of solution, when order is again restored to a society that is made more aware of some moral value or revolutionary thought. When social or literary conventions, even thought processes, do not lead to civility, order, or morality, they need to be moderated, even restructured. Unless these changes take place, the chaos that results from murder and from murder unsolved will prevail. Intellect, compassion, imagination, and wit are some of the possible routes to a reordering of society.

Such concerns can also be found in the fictive universe of Dorothy Sayers, the English writer of detective novels par excellence, a scholar of medieval literature at Oxford. "It is impossible," Heilbrun writes, "to overestimate the importance of her detective novels in my life. . . . I read Sayers and through her wit, her intelligence, her portrayal of a female community and a moral universe, I caught sight of a possible life" (*WWL,* 51–52). At the celebration of the fiftieth anniversary of the publication of *Gaudy Night,* one of Sayers's best novels set in Oxford, Heilbrun addressed a conference at Somerville College, where Sayers had studied, concerning the influence of the novel on American women readers. Sayers, also a feminist, is often quoted by Kate Fansler.

Other writers of detective fiction important to Heilbrun are the English writers Agatha Christie; Michael Gilbert, whose *Smallbone Deceased* she delights in rereading; P. D. James; Josephine Tey; and John le Carré. The Americans she prefers are Sara Paretsky, Sue Grafton, and Tony Hillerman. She no longer enjoys the novels of Ngaio Marsh, but Heilbrun admits that at one time she was much influenced by her.

Readers of the Amanda Cross novels will find that plot is never a key ingredient, while character often is. "What is distinctive in the Amanda Cross canon is her irony," writes Steven R. Carter in *Ten Women of Mystery,* "her ability to construct a mystery around the ideas of a single literary or intellectual figure, her application of her research on androgyny and a feminist history, the increasing complexity and appeal of her detective Kate Fansler, her responsiveness to the crises of her time."[2] Also distinctive are Heilbrun's many allusions to literature, most often British, and her use of facile and probingly intelligent conversation. The dialogue in these novels reminds some critics of the British playwright Noel Coward's—witty and sparkling.

Overview of the Novels

The first of the five novels discussed in chapter 4 is *In the Last Analysis,* which focuses on the murder of one of Kate Fansler's students. Here Freudian psychoanalysis is employed—and considered as effective as deductive logic—in solving the crime. One of the themes that emerges in this first novel will recur in those that follow: a character of integrity cannot commit a crime. The next novel, *The James Joyce Murder,* employs all of the story titles in Joyce's *Dubliners* as chapter titles. Here a murder in a quiet hamlet shatters the appearance of peace and tranquility.

Poetic Justice, which revolves around the metropolitan campus where Fansler teaches, concerns the unintended death of a professor of English by a colleague who is elegant, articulate, and scholarly. Some critics believe this fictional figure resembles Lionel Trilling. One theme suggested is the crumbling of morality that transpires when intellect and urbanity are misused. Another is the imperative of change.

The fourth detective book, *The Theban Mysteries,* set in a private high school for girls, employs the *Antigone* theme of resistance to authority as it deals with a Vietnam draft resister, the generation gap, and the relevance of the famous Greek classic to modern times. Although there is an assumption of homicide, none occurs. Individuality versus the concerns of a community constitute one of the novel's themes.

Heilbrun's fifth detective story, *The Question of Max*, revolves around a charming and gifted professor and colleague of Fansler, one who, unlike another educator in *Poetic Justice*, commits murder intentionally and then even attempts to kill Fansler. Some critics also seem to think this character resembles Trilling. The malefactor commits forgery and murder to conceal his identity and condemnatory information. Greed and hypocrisy are among the themes explored in this potently feminist novel.

In the Last Analysis

The plot of *In the Last Analysis* revolves around the murder of Janet Harrison, who was stabbed on the couch of the psychoanalyst Emanuel Bauer, a close friend and former lover of Kate Fansler. Harrison, a former student of Fansler, had asked her professor to recommend a therapist and Fansler suggested Bauer. Bauer is now under suspicion of murder, and Fansler, a professor of English literature at a private metropolitan university, is impelled to help him. After some hedging, she seeks the assistance of Reed Amhearst, an assistant district attorney whom she had helped out some time ago. Amhearst appears in all of the Cross novels and eventually becomes Kate's husband. At one point, via an anonymous letter, Fansler is accused of murdering Harrison—for a number of reasons, including the false charge of plagiarizing Harrison's work. There are no clues given to the reader along the way, but the murderer is finally discovered to be one Dr. Michael Barrister—or, more accurately, the murderer of Dr. Barrister. This man killed Barrister and then assumed his identity. When Harrison, who had been in love with the real Barrister, recognized the phony Barrister as an imposter, he killed her.

Virtually the only character reflecting any development in the novel is Kate Fansler, who is portrayed as clever, imaginative, and persistent, with an unremitting belief in the innocence of Emanuel Bauer. In a conversation with Reed Amhearst, Kate explains her support of her friend. "Emanuel, and others like him, love their work; and if you want my recipe for integrity, find the man who loves his work and loves the cause he serves."[3] Fansler, too, loves university teaching, English literature, and her students. She recalls a line from one of her favorite novels, George Eliot's *Middlemarch:* "'Strange that some of us, with quick alternate vision, see beyond our infatuations, and even while we rave on the heights, behold the wide plain where our persistent self pauses and awaits us'" (*LA,* 67). Because Emanuel possesses "the persistent self" integrally associated with complete immersion in work, he has to be helped or saved, thinks Fansler. This idea, among other insights, enriches an otherwise traditional detective novel and reflects the character of Fansler.

In this same part of the book, chapter 7, Fansler, in talking with a student who might have known the murder victim, says, "In the solution of a murder, Kant's *categorical imperative* had continually to be ignored" (*LA,* 68–69). *Webster's New Collegiate Dictionary* defines the categorical imperative as "a moral obligation or command that is unconditionally and universally binding."[4] In other words, in the probing of a murder investigation, the usual rules of conduct may not apply—to people or to circumstances or to evidence. This insight, too, rescues the novel from the pedestrian as it demonstrates Heilbrun's erudition.

Fansler almost uses the virtues of Bauer and to a lesser extent those of Amhearst as an objective correlative—both men possessing a high level of intelligence and integrity. When finding both virtues in the same person, concludes Fansler, "you have found a prize" (*LA,* 27).

In the Last Analysis, of course, since Fansler is an academic, she often ruminates on university professors and teaching. During her search for the murderer, Fansler attends a party attended by academics from an urban public college. This occasion provides the author with a chance to train her sights on professors, one of whom, admittedly, had he courage, would say, "You idiots, don't give me tenure; I am already dreadfully inclined to indolence, lassitude, self-indulgence and procrastination. You have enough dead wood in this benighted institution, enough minds which have not been penetrated by a new thought since the possibility of nuclear fission filtered through" (*LA,* 103). Such comments, abrasively witty, are often balanced by thought in favor of academicians, for elsewhere Fansler laments that "while the faculty is the only thing without which you cannot have a first-rate institution, it is the last element considered here" (*LA,* 105).

Psychoanalysis, another element that informs the novel in plot and character, falls into the range in which Cross often alludes to Freud. Early in the novel Fansler says she has no quarrel with Freud: "It's the dissemination of his ideas in the modern world" (*LA,* 5). In chatting with Amhearst, Fansler mentions the Freudian concept of the unconscious mind. The murderer, also in the scene, then makes a passing remark that reveals he knew the victim, Janet Harrison, a detail that, metaphorically, begins to tighten the noose around his neck.

One of Fansler's insights concerns the mind of a murderer—one that would possess a sadistic streak and the ability to look at people exclusively as obstacles to be removed. This underscores the author's use of character as a means of resolving a person's guilt or innocence.

This first detective novel in the Amanda Cross series elicited a flurry of critical comment. It was nominated in the best first novel category for the Edgar Award (named after Edgar Allan Poe) by the Mystery Writers of America. The nomination made Heilbrun uneasy, since the prize, as she has stated in several interviews, would have "blown her cover." Happily, she did not win the award but would be given a number of accolades in the future for her writing of mysteries.

Rebecca R. Butler says that in this first novel Kate Fansler demonstrates a sparkling wit and a searing intelligence. And the stereotypical sex roles are rejected. "A certain Noel Cowardesque conversational flair is a hallmark of the Cross mystery," she adds, and the sharp acuity of Fansler shows her to be "a stimulating teacher, a successful detective, and a good friend."[5]

Another critic, Steven R. Carter, who would come to write generally enthusiastic critiques of the Cross detective novels, has limited praise for this first one. "This puzzle is an end in itself; the solution to it makes the conventional point that order—personal, social and moral—can be restored through reason." He concludes that this novel is minor. "It succeeds in its aims, but its aims are limited" (270–71).

The James Joyce Murder

In *The James Joyce Murder,* the second Amanda Cross novel, published in 1967, the puzzle, buttressed by circumstances and not by psychology, is completely conventional. Kate Fansler, here a specialist in Victorian literature, goes to the Berkshires in Massachusetts in response to a request by Sam Lingerwell's daughter, now a nun, to edit letters from James Joyce to Lingerwell, deceased, who had been a publisher of James Joyce and D. H. Lawrence. She hires two Ph.D. students from her university, Emmet Crawford and William Lenehan, the former to aid in cataloguing and arranging the letters, and the latter to tutor her nephew Leo, who because of his recalcitrant nature needs a vacation from his parents. Reed Amhearst visits Fansler while on vacation from the attorney general's office.

Wealthy Sam Lingerwell, who left everything to his daughter, is modeled on Benjamin Huebsch, founder of the Viking Press, who published D. H. Lawrence early in his career. In an interview with Diana Cooper-Clark in *Designs of Darkness,* Heilbrun says, "I went to school with one of his sons. Huebsch was one of the great men of publishing, he and Knopf. . . . He was courageous and fine. I was extremely fond of him."[6]

Many mornings in the novel, William Lenehan and Leo go to the attic with an empty gun and aim at Mary Bradford, a self-righteous termagant and prurient town gossip. One day, she is shot and killed by Lenehan, who denies having put a bullet in the gun. With considerable help by Amhearst, a clever ruse reveals Lenehan to be the killer; his fury had erupted when Mary Bradford threatened to reveal his theft of a Joyce manuscript and blackmailed him into performing a sex act.

Several people are "red herrings"—that is, distractions that turn the reader's attention away from the real culprit—especially Padraic Mulligan, who was promoted to full professor despite his lackluster critical books. Actually, Mulligan writes under the nom de plume of Frank Held when his trashy "thrillers" are published. The publisher accepts the mediocre scholarly manuscripts because the thrillers sell in huge quantities. The publish-or-perish syndrome becomes one of the themes in the novel.

Significant in appreciating this novel, dominated, of course, by James Joyce, is familiarity with his work. The reader is advised to note that all 15 of the detective novel's chapters are titles of short stories in Joyce's collection *Dubliners.* "Araby," title of chapter 5, for instance, is the locale of the novel. Heilbrun also uses the names of Joyce characters for some of those in the novel, sometimes mixing in the name of a person from real life. "Red herring" Padraic Mulligan seems to be a combination of Buck Mulligan, a character in Joyce's *Ulysses,* and the late Padraic Colum, who was a professor of Irish literature at Columbia University.

In this novel, Reed Amhearst (whose name purportedly derives from those of two well-known colleges) upstages Kate Fansler in the solution of the puzzle. Reed is also fleshed out beyond the rough sketch in the first Cross novel. Here he is described by Mr. Farrell, a publisher, who says, "Your clothes were Brooks Brothers, your manners Groton, your ideas Stevensonian (Adlai, that is), and . . . you looked like an extremely attenuated Trevor Howard with glasses."[7] Farrell continues: "Justice [Standard] White described you as a man of few frivolities. I gather you read every word in the *Times,* enjoy an occasional decorous evening at the Plaza and go to the movies and theater from time to time" (*JJM,* 168).

Both Kate Fansler and Reed Amhearst indulge in considerably more badinage here than in the previous novel. And, although Reed may be a savvy lawyer, he provides some humor when he fails to recognize the titles of James Joyce's *Portrait of an Artist* and D. H. Lawrence's *The Rainbow*, thinking them to be paintings. Humor is also more prevalent in this novel, with the investigating detective the butt of many jokes.

Araby seems at first to be a bucolic, peaceable, even romantic kingdom, providing Reed with the environment to propose marriage to Kate. She rejects his offer, saying, "Reed, I am certain you don't realize what a selfish unwomanly, undomestic creature I am. I don't want to take care of anybody, really, or be the angel in the house!" (*JJM*, 50). She goes on to express her wish that they be together as the fancy takes them, "rather two circles, as Rilke said, which touch each other" (*JJM*, 51).

Two other women professors are invited to Araby—Grace Knole, a retired medieval scholar, who jokes about her age, and a younger one, Eveline Chisana, infatuated and even obsessed with Lenehan and disappointed that he does not make love to her. Professor Knole characterizes Kate: "You have many drawbacks, I don't mind telling you, and your inability to accept a compliment is certainly one of them. Also, you're somewhat less than a mountain of tact, you're impatient with brainlessness and the throwing of weight, and while you have the greatest respect for manners and courtesy, you have none at all for the proprieties as such" (*JJM*, 131). Despite these charges, Knole suggests that Fansler agree to be considered for the presidency of Jay College for Women. Fansler categorically refuses, even though Knole says that this job is a position of power, and "Power is one of the most remarkable experiences there is" (*JJM*, 132). Fansler demurs to wanting power, and Grace rounds off the discussion with, "I know that. Exactly why you should take it, rather than someone who has always wanted [power]" (*JJM*, 133).

The author projects many of her ideas, reactions, and commentaries on the immediate scene and her philosophic speculation onto Grace Knole, and she bestows on Grace some individuality. Her remarks range over such topics as rural life and crimes of a metaphoric mind to the nature of appearance and reality. On the other hand, all three professors, except occasionally for Evelina, the eighteenth-century specialist who has physical pleasures, mostly sex, on her mind, sound alike. They are quick-witted, sprightly, and enjoy the high art of conversation.

Only Fansler knows James Joyce well, and with Reed, the detectives, the other professors, and anyone else who listens, Kate shares her detailed knowledge of the Irish genius. One of the problems with Heilbrun's use of James Joyce throughout the novel is that she makes practically no thematic connection with *Dubliners,* whose theme is paralysis. The Cross book is focused primarily on murder and only secondarily on rural life, its charms and limitations, including lack of privacy and an implicit skirmishing between the year-round townspeople and seasonal residents, which include an enclave of educated, sophisticated people whose witty conversation is often made at the expense of the locals. A thin tissue of connection with the Joycean references appears in Heilbrun's portrayal of the deadliness and paralysis of conventional sexual morality, exemplified by the overwrought beliefs in virginity (or chastity) held by William Lenehan. Yet the novel envelops the reader more fully through its wide range of conversational gambits, the repeated allusions to James Joyce and his writings, and the burgeoning friendship of Kate Fansler and Reed Amhearst.

Steven R. Carter feels the novel is too derivative from "writers like Sayers, Marsh and Stout. . . . It is clearly an early novel, less innovative, less provocative, and less complex than subsequent ones, though not lacking the distinctive Amanda Cross voice and intellectual ambiance" (273).

Another critic, Melvin J. Friedman, writes of *The James Joyce Murder,* "It is a superior mystery and at the same time manages to say interesting things about the literary mentality."[8]

Poetic Justice

Poetic Justice, the third Amanda Cross novel, set in Manhattan, with much of the action taking place on Kate Fansler's metropolitan campus, confronts the riot and political unrest that characterized campus life in the late 1960s. (In fact, there was a riot of several days at Columbia University when all academic activity stood still and students battled with the police; even professors were arrested for having interfered with a police action merely by being in the vicinity.)

The novel examines the views and actions of the faculty, administration, and some few students in the aftermath of that "revolution." In novelistic art as in reality, the academic world would never be the same again. One of the concerns at the core of the novel is the questionable respectability of the undergraduate University College, where untraditional students, often those with full-time jobs, or whose education had been interrupted, could earn a degree. The novel portrays a gamut of university professors, of whom all are men except for Kate Fansler and

Emilia Airhart (a weak play on the famous pilot's name), who politically
skirmish over the continuation of University College. Heilbrun casts
many barbs at the students of the undergraduate college, where traditionally only males were accepted, students whose arrogance, indolence,
and often borderline academic performance are cosseted by certain professors, among them Jeremiah Cudlipp and Frederick Clemance, who, if
this book is a roman à clef, is a mirror image of Lionel Trilling, mentioned at length in the first chapter. Clemance, of course, is opposed to
the continuance of University College.

Scattered liberally throughout *Poetic Justice* is the poetry of W. H.
Auden (1907–73), English-born close friend of Christopher Isherwood.
Reed Amhearst, Kate, and Clemance quote Auden's verse, which also
serves to create an epigraph for each chapter.

The death in the novel (not technically a murder) is that of Jeremiah
Cudlipp, chair of the Graduate English Department, who was violently
opposed to the continuation of University College because he felt that
this branch diluted the value of the college's degree. His death does not
occur until page 94 of the novel's 169. Cudlipp's demise takes place on
the day of the faculty's celebration of the engagement of Kate Fansler
and Reed Amhearst, who plan to marry on Thanksgiving Day because it
will be easy to remember anniversaries. When Cudlipp complains of a
severe headache, Clemance brings him water. As Cudlipp collapses, he
cries, "Aspirin!"[9] Amhearst and others rush him down the college elevator, which stalls, a circumstance that contributes to his demise. A number of people knew that the victim was allergic to aspirin and had his
medication (aspirin-free) sent from England. They become suspects.

Amhearst primarily unravels the facts surrounding Cudlipp's death,
while Fansler, deeply sympathetic to the cause of University College,
pursues clues and anyone who might have substituted the aspirin. The
perpetrators are suspected to be those supporting the untraditional
University College or anyone else who despised the emotionally charged,
rude, and dyspeptic Cudlipp.

Clemance, who ignored Kate Fansler when she had been his student
and virtually overlooked her as colleague as well, begins to seek her out
for many reasons, one of which is to ask her to join a dissertation committee for a student writing on Auden's poetry and also to determine her
views regarding University College. Fansler and Clemance indulge in
several pointed conversations. "Miss Fansler, could your University
College have produced Auden?" "No. And neither could your College,
Professor Clemance" (*PJ*, 58).

Earlier, Fansler had agreed with Clemance when he suggested that she considered him prejudiced. This prejudice includes in fact anti-feminism, since Clemance prefers the College, which admits only males. A short time later Clemance further confirms his male chauvinism by recalling that as his student, Kate wrote a paper on Henry James's *Portrait of a Lady*. He says, "I have never especially cared for women students. I think perhaps I was wrong in that. Perhaps there are Isabel Archers at University College" (*PJ,* 59). (The center of consciousness in this novel by James is Isabel Archer.)

Just as Carolyn Heilbrun acknowledged her debt to Lionel Trilling in teaching her an interpretation of literature, so too does Kate Fansler admit to Clemance her gratitude. "Professor Clemance, I have often wished for the opportunity to tell you that you taught me more—about literature, something I can only call morality, and about the honor of the profession of letters—than anyone else in the University" (*PJ,* 59). She also asserts that he seems to prefer young male acolytes and not someone like her, an older female disciple. Their lengthy conversation virtually characterizes Clemance, who admits that his heart has been broken by the student revolt. There is, of course, irony in Kate's use of "morality," given the subsequent events surrounding the death of Cudlipp.

Well into *Poetic Justice* Clemance invites Kate and Reed to accompany him to a campus reading by Auden of his poetry. Known as "the University's most renowned adornment," Clemance for many reasons becomes a key character, but especially because Cudlipp's death resulted from Clemance's having given him the aspirin. The faulty elevator that delayed his arrival at the hospital, only three blocks away, was the coup de grâce. Reed mistakenly assumed during his investigation of the murder that someone placed the aspirin in Cudlipp's bottle. The solution revolves around a slip of the tongue. Clemance tells Reed that "there are moments when, quite apart from wanting Cudlipp back again, I wish that someone had handed me a poison, instead of him" (*PJ,* 104). With this remark, Reed knows Cudlipp took the pills from Clemance's hands and that Clemance had substituted the aspirin. Clemance hastens to add that it was not his intention to murder his colleague but only to frighten him, to urge him to control his outbursts and to relax his iron grip on administrative power. In tandem with Clemance's serious wrongdoing was the collusion of Cudlipp's students, who were urged by Clemance to tamper with the elevators and to foment unrest in the University, an act of consummate irony, since the stalled elevator contributed to the death of the English department's chair.

A theme recapitulated in the novel probes the students' anger, impatience, and perceptions that galvanized the university riots. Fansler, attending the Auden reading, hears the poet speak about the primary world (that in which we exist) and the secondary world (the world of art); both worlds must have rules. "It occurred to Kate, thinking of the present university situation of turmoil, to wonder whether the secondary worlds the revolutionaries were trying to create were not, so far, dangerously lawless." Did young people realize the need for law? Auden says that unrestricted freedom is without meaning. People are free to determine the laws, but once they are in place, must they not be obeyed? All of these insights, like atoms colliding and energizing one another, spin from the reading and commentary of Auden.

The results of the student groundswell have shaken the faculty to the core, caused a radical curriculum revision, and, at the end of the novel, secured the continuance of University College, with the concomitant promotion of professors teaching in that division. Negative results also occur—bickering within and between departments, irrelevant course substitutions, irrational questioning of power structures, and the faculty fatigue and fear of implementing questionable innovations.

When Clemance tells Fansler that "your University College" may have a new lease on life, Fansler retorts that in wondering why she showed passion in this crusade, "I suspect I was outraged at those who didn't want their status symbols interfered with. I mean, it was so clear the fight wasn't over academic excellence, but over snobbery and a wicked kind of prejudice" (*PJ*, 157).

Since Clemance's power and prestige are portrayed as iconic and his ethical concerns in literature well known and meritorious, his putting of Cudlipp at severe risk in handing him the aspirin is sharply ironic. Clemance himself senses the enormity of his act. "We cannot guess the outcome of our actions—how often I have said that in discussions with students. Which is why our actions must always be acceptable in themselves; and not as strategies" (*PJ*, 158). Nevertheless, Clemance seems to justify his action by subsequently revealing that Cudlipp was probably certifiably mad and that he, along with other faculty, actually cracked from the stress of the spring revolt.

What may seem astonishing to some readers is Reed's attitude toward Clemance's moral turpitude. Reed tells Clemance he will not cover up his involvement but will not publicize it; rather, he will file an account of "how you must have given Cudlipp the aspirin; an accident will be assumed, and indeed, his death was an accident if I know the definition of the word" (*PJ*, 161). Neither he nor Kate later discusses the fall from grace of a professor who espoused morality in literature and who in real life violated his precept and virtually negated his entire philosophy of life. "The rest is silence," from *Hamlet*, might be the coda of the professional and the amateur detectives concerning Clemance.

Despite the seriousness of its substance, the novel does employ humor, even frivolity. One of the most amusing scenes takes place in the University basement when Reed, poised on a water pipe, waits in darkness for the culprit who meddled with the elevators. In the same basement scene, when one professor mistakenly sprays another with water, both also searching for the miscreant, hilarity results. Acerbic humor is also shown when Dean Robert O'Toole congratulates Fansler on her upcoming marriage and says, "All women should be married. An unmarried woman is an offense against nature" (*PJ*, 89). Kate, deeply offended, is searching for a reply when Emilia Airhart comes to her rescue by saying, "What I can never understand about you, Mr. O'Toole, is whether you think arrogant bad manners encourage the illusion of manliness, or whether you think that evident unmanliness is somehow obscured by arrogant bad manners" (*PJ*, 90). Names also provide some levity—Professor Peter Packer Pollinger, Jeremiah Cudlipp, Dean Vivian Frogmore, and, of course, Emilia Airhart.

The conversations between Reed and Kate throughout the book are filled with badinage. Kate tells her fiancé, "You know, Reed, I think if you'd only come to a Department party earlier, and let me see you, beautifully lanky and relaxed among all those professors, I would have proposed long ago. Would you have accepted?" (*PJ*, 97). Reed replies, "Probably with a lot less trepidation than I have now. You know, Kate, I've never really minded your being a sort of overage Nancy Drew" (*PJ*, 97).

The combination of earnestness and frivolity is a mirror image of many of Auden's poetic motifs. Auden, at the University reading, says, "The life of a poet is a balancing act between frivolity and earnestness"; Kate muses that this sentiment expresses Auden's brilliance. "He is the best balancer of all" (*PJ*, 156). Steven Carter declares, "*Poetic Justice* aims at the same kind of balance—and achieves it. The vision of the novel accords perfectly" with several lines from the Auden poem—quoted in the novel (*PJ*, 53)—that suggests laughter is less heartless than tears.

Festooned as the novel is with the Auden's poetry, some readers may be inspired to study more of his poetry and life; others may tire of the many quotations. Carol Cleveland, in *Twentieth Century Crime and Mystery*

Writers, comments, "If the poet were not Auden, there would be too much of it."[10]

Another critic, J. M. Purcell, in *The Armchair Detective,* praises the "fascinating" idea of using Lionel Trilling as a villain in the novel, but says the author "fails to invent for her fictional 'Trilling' a criminal act or moral offense that will articulate whatever serious criticism she is making of him." Purcell then adds that although the novel has a veneer of sophistication, "we find some taint of amateurism in bread-and-butter matters of plot and theme."[11]

Although Amanda Cross uses the gentle art of Horatian satire in her portrayals of a gaggle of university professors, the theme almost cries out for a parody of the fossils that some faculty have become. Yet the satire and deadly wit of a Jonathan Swift or even of a Lord Byron are absent. Clemance escapes even a metaphoric guillotining.

The Theban Mysteries

In 1971, one year following the publication of *Poetic Justice, The Theban Mysteries* appeared. The Theban School, a hundred years old, founded by Matthias Theban to educate his four daughters properly, is the Manhattan secondary private school that Kate Fansler herself had attended.

Fansler is implored by Miss Tyringham, the head of Theban, to lead a senior seminar on the *Antigone* of Sophocles, the Greek dramatist, since one of the teachers has suffered a slipped disc. At first reluctant because she is on leave from her university, Kate demurs, but eventually agrees to substitute at her alma mater.

The novel covers a range of topics—the faculty, the students and their attitudes, concepts of education, the generation gap, the Vietnam War, the *Antigone* seminar, security at the school, and the discovery of a dead parent in the art room. Fansler and her husband, Reed, combine their wits to unravel the mystery of the death of Esther Jablon, mother of Angelica, a student in Fansler's seminar. No murder occurs in this novel; Mrs. Jablon dies of a heart attack. Mr. O'Hara, who handles security with help from his two Doberman pinschers, Rose and Lily, is a distinctive figure. His two guard dogs are trained to step on pads if all is secure. Nothing appeared amiss the night before the body was discovered; therefore, it was obvious that Mrs. Jablon had died elsewhere and was moved to the Theban.

Kate's investigation reveals that Mrs. Jablon, a neurotic harridan, had intruded on her daughter's encounter group, where she was met with a hateful response from Angelica. Mrs. Jablon becomes so enraged that she suffers a heart attack and dies. Mrs. Banister, the drama teacher, with the help of a student, transports the body to the Theban.

The themes of *Antigone,* examined in the seminar by Kate Fansler, are woven into the thematic structure of the novel. In Sophocles' drama, Antigone, daughter of Oedipus of Thebes, flagrantly disobeys the order of Creon, her uncle, and buries the body of her brother out of filial love and moral duty. She is then sentenced to death by Creon. He later lifts the death sentence, but it is too late; Antigone has committed suicide. Those readers familiar with the Greek tragedy know that after Antigone's death, Creon's son, loving Antigone, commits suicide, as does his mother at grief over her son's death. This play's themes concern conflicting obligations—duty to the state (Creon's law) versus religious mores and personal loyalty, *hubris* (overweening presumption), and compromise.

Antigone's themes are discussed by Fansler and her seminar group, young women who seem brighter than many college students. They constantly challenge Fansler, who limits her role as leader. In this novel, Fansler shows considerable tolerance for young people, as she did not in *Poetic Justice.* These discussions, provocative and illuminating, elicit thought-provoking ideas about not only the Greek play but also a number of moral issues.

When one young woman attacks Creon as a tyrant, Fansler insists that there *is* some right on his side, that George Eliot believed in this play "the conflict is between individual judgment and the conventions of society, but it is dangerous to assume that the conventions of society are, despite our sneering use of the word 'conventional,' necessarily wrong."[12] Lacking these conventions, every day would need to be a new beginning back in time.

So gifted is Betsy Stark, one student in the seminar, that she decides to read Jean Anouilh's *Antigone,* published in 1944, which in occupied France was permitted to be performed because the Nazis believed Creon was right and that Antigone, who represented the Free French, was wrong. Anouilh's play stresses the limits of employing compromise to achieve happiness; of course, even in his play, Antigone rejects compromise.

Angelica Jablon, also a seminar student, introduces the theme of Antigone as woman. "Antigone had to be a woman; it's why Creon can keep sneering at her. 'No woman's going to tell me what to do' and that sort of thing. Only a woman was enough of a slave to like require the kind of guts Antigone had" (*TM,* 57). Kate adds that Virginia Woolf, too, suggests this idea, more or less.

Correlative to the issue of Antigone's womanhood is that of Tiresias, the blind seer in the play, who attempts to persuade Creon to compromise. It is the clever Betsy who articulates the view—also expressed by Heilbrun in *Toward a Recognition of Androgyny*—that Tiresias is an androgynous figure. "Tiresias had actually been both a man and a woman," says Betsy, and "so was the only person who could report on what it was like to be both sexes, an enviable position, was it not?" (*TM,* 58). Kate marvels at Betsy's intellectual abilities and thinks that she could become something if she doesn't press too hard and burn out. Fansler does not like teaching the very young because there seems to be unending potential, yet "most of it is gone before they get their wisdom teeth" (*TM,* 58).

Integrated into these discussions of the Greek play is the leitmotif of Vietnam. Fansler's nephew Jack and Angelica's brother Patrick both oppose the draft. Their actions mirror some of the themes in *Antigone*—such as individual rebellion against the state. Both Jack's father and Patrick's grandfather strenuously oppose the moral attitudes of their progeny.

The male character most fully and convincingly portrayed, with much poignancy, is Patrick's grandfather, Cedric Jablon, a Jew who had immigrated to America penniless and then amassed a fortune in his adopted country. Kate and Jablon have long discussions about his coming to America, his grandson's draft evasion, and the *Antigone* seminar. About the play, Jablon says, "I discover that your play is an excuse for betraying one's country" (*TM,* 83). He further protests: "What all these young people, with their dirty clothes and rioting seem to be doing; they are trying to escape their destiny, which is to work and have respect for their elders and their country and learn something" (*TM,* 84). Kate, who throughout has argued that *Antigone* is a great play, tells him there are no oracles to inform us what is fated, not even a Tiresias. Chapter 6 contains one of the most poignant scenes in the novel in its allusions to Dante, betrayal, freedom of speech, and democracy. Jablon explains his concept of eternal truths, but Fansler says, "I don't think we agree on what are eternal truths, apart from the fact that man only learns at a terrible price and there are no easy answers" (*TM,* 85).

Jablon's litany of details on his arrival in the United States and his ordeals may remind the reader of Carolyn Heilbrun's father, who, like Jablon, arrived without a sou and became a millionaire. Fansler gently points out that his imperatives are moral absolutes, that Creon learns of the overcertainty of his decrees, "that he has overestimated the impor-

tance of law and order" (*TM*, 87). When Jablon feels he is too emotional
and wants to leave, Fansler tells him not to apologize for his feelings
"when you've something to be upset about. Why else be human, why
else love people" (*TM*, 88). She concludes their dialogue by saying that
he should come and visit her again if he doesn't mind a good fight. This
chapter especially characterizes Fansler as sharp-witted, honest and
direct, empathetic and wise, all qualities of a first-rate teacher and a
worthwhile human being.

Despite the depiction of Esther Jablon, Cedric's daughter-in-law, as a
hysterical, self-indulgent, hypochondriacal woman who is hoisted by her
own petard, Fansler believes that she reflects the position of many
women who are dependent on their husbands or (in this case) on her
father-in-law, that this necessity demeans women, damages their psy-
ches, and makes men feel guilty for holding them in thrall and wishing
to escape them. In Fansler's opinion, men "would never have had wars
throughout history if men had not needed an excuse to get away from
their wives" (*TM*, 134).

A war veteran and apparently a bachelor, O'Hara (who is not given a
first name), who provides the security for the Theban School, clearly dis-
likes women. Before Reed and Kate went to see him to discuss Mrs.
Jablon's death (he discovered the body), Kate wondered whether he
might resemble Heathcliff with his snarling dogs. When O'Hara did
meet them, "He seemed to find Kate, another female in an institution
already overflowing with them, superfluous, and waited with undis-
guised hope for Reed to bid her adieu at the doorway to the roof" (*TM*,
113). The misogyny of O'Hara, Kate thinks, does not apply to his
canines; he asks for a kiss from and then strokes Rose and Lily through
the wire barrier. O'Hara is incensed at the prevailing opinion that Mrs.
Jablon encountered the dogs at night, was terrified by them, and conse-
quently suffered a heart attack. In a hilarious scene, Ross cooperates by
facing the dogs like a "tethered goat" and proves that Rose and Lily will
not attack a living person if not provoked.

Another well-defined character is Miss Tyringham, the headmistress,
who is called a genius. "She turned out to possess exactly the right qual-
ifications for this odd job, having a highly organized mind, a flexible
attitude toward change and the amazing ability to talk about the problems of curriculum with parents' groups" (*TM*, 41–42). Wise pedagogue
that she is, Miss Tyringham does not flinch when honesty is needed. She
calls an assembly to explain to the student body the disturbing recent
happening in the school.

All in all, *The Theban Mysteries* confronts a wide range of themes, many of which are developed and which often intersect, although the mystery of the death is not sufficiently integrated with the *Antigone* theme.

Although Steven Carter generally admires the novel, he deplores the absence of a fuller treatment of the moral and psychological problems of the two Jablon children. Also, he laments that "forty to fifty pages are devoted exclusively to details like the movement of guard dogs, the location of elevators, the identification of a tie label and the medical history of the deceased" (292).

Another critic, Rebecca R. Butler in *Critical Survey of Mystery and Detective Fiction,* writes that in *The Theban Mysteries,* "The model of ratiocination is Kate's *Antigone* seminar, a beautifully crafted conversation of a special kind which illustrates the art of deciding what is worth examining" (428). Finally, Newgate Callendar found the novel gentle and thoughtful, the writing "literate, low-keyed, sophisticated."[13]

The Question of Max

The fifth novel in the Amanda Cross series, *The Question of Max,* appearing in 1976, was for many critics the most successful of the first five in its merging of plot puzzle and theme. Commentators praised the plot for its density, tightness, and plausibility; for some, this novel is a masterpiece. The main character, Max Reston, a colleague of Kate Fansler, is seamlessly sculptured. Once more, as in *In the Last Analysis,* the polarity of character and the level of morality determine innocence or guilt.

Max Reston appears uninvited at a pastoral cabin used as a retreat by Kate Fansler from urban and academic stress. "A professor of art history, Max was renowned for his achievements as a scholar and his elegance as a bachelor and man about town."[14] He begs Fansler to accompany him on a drive to the Maine house of the novelist Cecily Hutchins, now deceased. He has been made literary executor by Cecily, his mother's friend, there has been a break-in, and he does not drive.

Reston's social and intellectual snobbery, together with his conservatism, is immediately apparent. He is widely disliked and envied, but his saving grace of befriending those of whom he approves tempers his self-centeredness and eccentricity. Over the years, Kate has developed "profound affection" for him and a measure of trust. At the imposing country house of Cecily, built on a meadow close to the cliffs overlooking the sea, the spirit of the novelist, born in England, dominates. When

Kate and Max stroll near the promontory, Kate decides to clamber down the rocks alone. At the bottom she finds a dead body, face down, submerged in a pool of the tides.

When the body is taken to the police station and shown to her and Max, Kate is horrified to recognize her student Gerry Marston, who, she later recalled, was writing a dissertation on Dorothy Whitmore, a dear friend of Cecily whose picture hangs over the fireplace in Cecily's home. To Fansler, Dorothy appears "young, blond, marvelously agreeable looking" (*QM,* 30). Cecily Hutchins, Dorothy Whitmore, and Frederica Tupe Reston, Max's mother, were all students at Oxford University, England, in 1920.

Although on the discovery of the corpse Max says nothing, he later tells Kate that several days previously he found Gerry Marston had broken into the house and that when they walked to the cliff, she stumbled and fell to her death. Eventually, on a trip to Oxford, Kate reads through the letters and novels of Dorothy Whitmore and, when returning, reads through more letters by her to conclude that Max is the illegitimate son of Dorothy Whitmore. She tells Max, who admits to having killed Marston to keep the secret of his ignoble birth.

Eventually, Fansler perceives that Max manipulated her through a series of forged letters to arrive at the wrong motive for the murder; quite by chance, she finds out details from a student, changing the picture of Max's complicity. Max finally reveals that Cecily and he did not agree on many matters and that she had intended to alter her will, but never did. Marston discovered this, and so Max killed her. In the final pages of the book, Max is about to kill Kate and then disguise the murder as a suicide.

The Question of Max, like its four predecessors, does not fit strictly into the detective genre but rather becomes a mystery of manners, the mystery ancillary to the manners. The themes combine misogyny, feminism, hubris, educational scams, administrative venality, betrayal, courage, and certainly self-revelation, that moment of sober epiphany.

Max Reston becomes the hub around which the novel revolves, and although he is sophisticated, charming at times, rational, refined, and intelligent, his actions also reveal him to be aggressive, sinister, self-righteous, manipulative, misogynistic, and acquisitive. He is a liar, forger, and killer. When the forged letters point to Max's illegitimacy, he continues to befog the real issue by letting Kate believe his mother was Dorothy Whitmore, whom he viciously attacks. "Who would want a mother, however goddesslike, a feminist, a freethinker, a socialist and a pacifist. It's everything I loathe. . . . I like women to be ladies, wives, and mothers, or at worst, eccentric and appealing old maids" (*QM*, 181).

In reading a batch of letters forged by Max, Kate concludes that Dorothy Whitmore, expecting a child, hopes it will be a boy, "'with his destiny clear and sharp before him. Isn't it odd that none of us longs for daughters?'" (*QM*, 191). Kate, despite her acute intellect, is temporarily blinded by her hubris and does not sense that a true feminist would not hope so intently for a male child.

In the final scene with Max Reston, who again comes to Kate's country retreat uninvited, she has learned that he is not illegitimate, that Whitmore was not his mother, and that Max has led her down the garden path. She berates him, "Have you come, Max, because it gives you pleasure to dote on what a fool I've been, and how easily you manipulated me?" (*QM*, 199). Kate proves herself to have been sharp-witted, however, in noting the forgery by comparing the typefaces of a letter from Marston to herself about the student's dissertation with a letter Marston supposedly wrote to Cecily. She also tells Max that Whitmore would never have wished for a boy and that women are not as self-loathing as he assumes.

Again, Max reveals his misogyny when he recalls for Kate his final visit to Cecily, who had, he said, turned into a flaming liberal. Cecily had told Max that she had to do everything for her husband, a painter (who had died several years earlier and whom she always called "Ricardo," his last name), that she always found herself massaging his ego. These details among others indicated that her marriage was an unhappy one. Max was dismissed, with Cecily saying, "You're wrong for me, as literary executor and certainly as biographer. I shall make that clear in my will" (*QM*, 207). The character of Max thus intersects with the theme of feminism in the final portion of the book.

In her excitement and speed to find the murderer of her student, Kate pursues all clues and eventually goes to Oxford to compile more background on Whitmore and to read her books there. Oxford to Fansler "was the hub of the scholar's universe" (*QM*, 129). This academic sanctuary, she muses, holds secrets—in the form of unfolding gardens and courts—known only to initiates. The novel alludes to many details of Oxford's glorious setting[15] and combines Fansler's detective expedition with a visit to her friends, Phyllis and her husband, Hugh, who is teaching a year at Oxford.

Phyllis laments that British men, especially at Oxford, keep their women in thrall and invite her husband out while she remains at home, as do all Oxford faculty wives. Kate receives a letter from home mentioning Robert Graves, who taught at Oxford and who married a feminist who was anti-religious because "God is a man, so it must be all rot" (*QM*, 145–46). Phyllis tells Kate that many of these men have as wives perfectly behaved servants. These two friends also discuss Kate's ideas and research, talking about Tupe, Hutchins, and Whitmore. Tupe had become only the wife of Reston. Cecily became a writer and reveled in her solitude and art, while Whitmore, having served in World War I with few women among the soldiers, pursued two ideas: "Women must cease thinking they were ordained by God to be servants, and she must increase her sense of that opportunity to live life" (*QM*, 152). Much of the history of these three women is given through narration, not drama, and this telling and not showing strains and slows the movement of this part of the novel.

Another important segment of the book revolves around Leo, who in *The James Joyce Murder* spends a summer in the country with his aunt, then unmarried. Leo Fansler reappears in this book and lives with Kate and Reed for a year while attending his senior year of high school at St. Anthony's. Some episodes involving Leo and Kate—her going to see him play in baseball and basketball games, the young man's direct (obscene) and pithy language, and his strong opinions—provide humor. Once he wanders into Kate's room and says, "'Let's hear a few bright remarks about Prufrock'" (*QM*, 55), the character in T. S. Eliot's "The Love Song of J. Alfred Prufrock." Kate knows enough about Leo and about young people to let them initiate conversations. Leo tells Kate, who objects to the cacophonous music before a basketball game, that the young people like it because it "psychs" up the team.

An important theme in the novel develops around a minor character—15-year-old Chet Ricardo. A student at St. Anthony's and the grandson of Cecily, he swaggers, womanizes, and takes drugs. After his SAT scores were sent to Harvard, he was accepted there, but it turns out that he had Finlay, a genius, take the exam for him. Leo, asking Kate and Reed what he should do about the cheating, believes he, like all the students who know, should do nothing, but he is very angry at the school's being so lax that students get away with taking exams for each other. The administration worries more about public relations than about the integrity and character of the student body. Reed makes a cogent remark when he discusses parents who advise their children not to get involved in such an ethical issue: "Righteousness is a very unpopular stand. We like people to do our dirty work for us, but

we reserve the right to call them moralistic bastards when they do"
(*QM*, 97).

Leo would like to tell the faculty what happened, and he mentions
the risk. Perhaps Ricardo and Finlay would kill those who told or plant
heroin on them and call the police. Reed and Kate stare in astonishment
at Leo, almost 18, who is already aware of the risk and the cost of
upholding the truth and the law. He is both adult and child in measur-
ing the danger and the fear of the consequences. The moral issues, which
are important in all of the mystery novels of Amanda Cross, are articulated by Reed, the lawyer, who discusses people fighting for law and
expecting thanks but being spit at instead. "You can only fight for law
because you think it is so important you're unable to do anything else"
((*QM*, 99). Reed, who, like Kate, is witty, ends by asking whether someone might like to hire him as a commencement speaker; his fees are low
and his style rambling.

Some St. Anthony students, including Leo, tell the faculty about the
cheating, stirring up a whole flurry of consequences: Harvard decides
that Ricardo and Finlay cannot attend this year; parents rush around the
school; most faculty think the matter has been ineptly handled; and the
headmaster makes some lame excuses. Kate empathizes with Leo and
says, "You decide to do something, perform one small action, and suddenly it's a tide, the momentum is going, and there's no possibility of
turning back. Somehow, even though you thought you foresaw all that
would happen, you didn't know the pace would pick up so. . . . To have
done nothing would have been worse" (*QM*, 194). Such is the moral
imperative that Amanda Cross projects in this and other novels, a quest
for justice, for order—the antithesis of the chaos that a murder and a
murderer create.

Still another theme resonates in this novel—that of androgyny. An
immediately perceived androgynous figure can be recognized in Tate
Sparrow (named after the Tate Gallery in London), the librarian of the
Wallingford, which received the Hutchins papers. He tells Kate that he
had first read Hutchins when he was 11. The novel was about a family
spending a summer in France. Tate reminisces, "'All girls, except for one
eleven-year-old boy, who was, of course, me. But before I was through, I
was all of them'" (*QM*, 103). He deplores those manly types crouched in
their hunt for animal flesh.

The androgynous ideal can be seen in other characters: Cecily
Hutchins and Dorothy Whitmore, who show an independent spirit,
unafraid to reveal and use their rationality, and who do not seek their

identification through men. And, of course, Reed Amhearst and Kate
Fansler also are recognizable androgynes. Reed is not fearful about but
rather relaxed with the "feminine traits in his personality and can casually admit that he is more emotionally dependent on Kate than she is on
him" (QM, 63). A few pages later he joshes Kate for her enthusiasm for
"manly" sports. That Kate Fansler is especially androgynous is almost a
given. She goes off alone to her country retreat, uses her gifted mind,
reveals her independent spirit throughout the novel, yet is sensitive to
the needs of others and unafraid to show emotion.

On the other hand, Ricardo and Max are "masculine-ideal" types,
grounded and limited by their social backgrounds and tradition in their
aggressiveness, competitiveness, solipsism, and feelings of superiority to
women. Ricardo cheats egregiously, uses women—even his famous
grandmother for his ambition to enter Harvard—and generally shows
cutthroat competitiveness in sports. An analysis of Max clearly reveals
his utter disregard for others—from his first visit to Kate in the country
to the last one, when he attempts to murder her. His use and abuse of
women make clear that he has no ameliorating feminine virtues.
President Nixon, frequently mentioned in the novel in connection with
Watergate, is portrayed in a way that underscores his lack of honor in his
obsession to win at any cost, a masculine trait fostered by society.

In "Interview with Amanda Cross" by Diana Cooper-Clark, the novelist reveals some pertinent details of *The Question of Max* that are rooted in
reality. The setting for the novel is that of the New England home of the
late poet, novelist, and essayist May Sarton, complete with a path to the
sea, very much like Cecily's. Heilbrun relates her walk down the rocks
with Sarton's Shetland collie, which she retraced in the novel by having
Kate traipse down the rocks while Max looked on. "I suddenly looked
back and I couldn't see land and there was the dog sinking in a sort of
pool with all that hair. I was afraid he would get wet and really sink
before I could pull him up. And I had a moment of almost blind panic.
That is what initiated *The Question of Max*. The body found there is a very
small moment in the story but that's where it started" (*Designs,* 195).

Heilbrun further relates how certain details of the childhood of Cecily
Hutchins were taken from that of Rose Macaulay, English novelist and
travel writer, whose books are characterized by social satire, intelligence,
and sprightly scholarship. Cecily and Dorothy in the novel were loosely
inspired by Vera Brittain, British author of *Testament of Friendship,* and
Winifred Holtby, British novelist, who left her estate to Somerville
College, as did Dorothy Whitmore. Both women, devoted friends, were

students at Oxford. (They appear in Heilbrun's *Writing a Woman's Life,* chapter 5, a book discussed in chapter 6 of this volume.)

The Question of Max received varying critiques, but most commentators found the plot tightly structured and plausible.

Rebecca R. Butler writes, "In *The Question of Max,* Cross achieved what some consider her greatest success in blending experimentation and tradition: she identifies the murderer from the beginning, the better to focus attention on that individual's character, social conditioning and misogynist motives. As she has gone about reshaping the detective story to suit her moral vision, feminism has remained foremost among the positions Cross champions" (428).

In his comments on *The Question of Max,* J. M. Purcell is incensed at the author's combining "summer resort atmosphere with a picture of Oxbridge contaminated by the venomous views of a visiting U.S. faculty wife who is under the misapprehension that she is better educated than the resident British faculty wives, and whose more idiotic views seem to be shared by the author" (36). He also writes that nonacademic professional readers of Amanda Cross might wonder at that after five novels, "Kate Fansler is professionally such a blank." He continues, "Kate seems to be doing the same research [in *The Question of Max*] that Dr. Heilbrun did for her doctoral *The Garnett Family* back in 1960; or perhaps the new 1976 *Lady Ottoline's Album.* What books has Kate published? What are her best students doing?" (40).

Steven Carter writes, "Cross's masterpiece, *The Question of Max,* achieves the harmonious blending of its disparate elements that is so unfortunately lacking in *The Theban Mysteries.*" He especially enjoyed the novel's "skillfully developed feminist/androgynous vision" (286).

No critic mentions or even hints that Max may have been inspired by Carolyn Heilbrun's Columbia University professor and colleague Lionel Trilling, known to be anti-feminist, snobbish, elegant of manner, and highly intellectual. Max Reston resembles the character of Frederick Clemance in *Poetic Justice,* in which book this character was compared by a number of critics with Trilling. In *The Question of Max,* however, Max is a vicious manipulator, whose heinous crimes and threat to Kate Fansler at the novel's end stir sheer disgust in the reader.

Finally, it is a matter of interest that Cross concludes her fifth novel with a passage on the photograph of Tupe, Hutchins, and Whitmore at Oxford in 1920. It is a tribute to those women who aspired and dared to attend Oxford, a male bastion in those days; these women were in effect breaking the sound barrier in university education.

Chapter Five

The Next Six Amanda Cross Mystery Novels

"Dabbling in revolutionary thought"

Overview of the Novels

Of all the Amanda Cross novels, the sixth, *Death in a Tenured Position,* is perhaps the best known and is for some fans the absolute best. Set at Harvard University, the action covers the apparent murder of Janet Mandelbaum, the first woman tenured by the all-male Department of English, which is depicted as rabidly anti-feminist. Heilbrun pummels the condescending elitism and bias against women observed at this prestigious university. *Sweet Death, Kind Death,* the seventh Cross novel, is pervaded by references to suicides of several famous women, including Virginia Woolf. The character Patrice Umphelby, another lone female tenured professor, in this case in the history department of a small New England college, is an apparent suicide, since she had spoken of not wanting to be invaded by old age. Kate unravels the mystery, which turns out to be a murder. An unusual angle in this book is its look at the unlimited possibilities of middle and old age.

No Word from Winifred, the eighth novel, is a mystery *sans* murder. Winifred Ashby disappears, and though Kate Fansler never meets her, she discovers in Winifred's journals a warm-spirited, independent woman who enjoys solitude and who meets the world, especially men, on her own terms. Descriptions of Oxford, England, portray the university town as a virtual Arcadia. Kate unravels the puzzle of the absent Winifred, who is sketched as one model of feminism.

The ninth Amanda Cross novel, *A Trap for Fools,* takes as its title a line from the famous Rudyard Kipling poem "If." A professor on Fansler's campus, an intensely disliked man, is murdered, and a black female student is murdered shortly thereafter. In uncovering the murderer, Kate herself is threatened and betrayed by a female friend. She also encounters problems on the campus—from corruption and racism to police bias and blackmail.

The tenth detective novel, *The Players Come Again,* takes its title from a line in Virginia Woolf's *The Waves.* It portrays a number of engaging women who had been close friends in their youth, pursued separate paths, and then resumed their close ties. Marriage, friendship, and feminism are important themes.

The eleventh novel, *An Imperfect Spy,* reverberates with quotes from English spy novelist John le Carré. The venue is Schuyler Law School in New York City. Kate and her husband, Reed, a lawyer, are hired for a semester, she to team-teach a course in literature and law. Before their arrival, a professor dies, and some believe she was murdered. Student unrest, resentments against women by male faculty (most of whom are mediocre), generational misunderstandings, wife battering, and the law's inequity toward women challenge Fansler and her husband, both of whom stir not only the interest but the anger of students. Once the two finish the semester, Schuyler Law School is never quite the same.

Death in a Tenured Position

The sixth novel in the Amanda Cross series, published in 1981, is one of its most popular, having received the Nero Wolfe Award for Mystery Fiction. What distinguishes *Death in a Tenured Position* from the previous five books is a clear frontal attack, a veritable laser beam of satire and anger, directed at Harvard University's idea of itself as the best university in the United States. Heilbrun also indicts the university for antifeminism and traditional patriarchal attitudes; when the novel was published there had not been one tenured woman on the faculty of the Department of English.

In an interview with Diane Cooper-Clark in 1983, Heilbrun says, "At the time I wrote *Death in a Tenured Position,* they'd never had one woman. Oddly enough, they have since appointed a woman in the same field as my fictional character. Life imitating art, once again."[1] Katha Pollitt, in reviewing the book, wrote, "I went to Harvard and was prepared from page 1 to cheer Cross's spirited dishing of my lamentably sexist alma mater. Said dishing is easily the book's best feature."[2]

Although *Death in a Tenured Position* is not so tightly plotted as *The Question of Max,* Cross breaks new ground this time by veering away from the classical mystery into a pure distillation of her thematic vision, her driving force of feminism.

Harvard's Department of English in this novel is an uncompromising bastion of male supremacy, unalterably opposed to having even a token

woman in its precinct until the hiring of Jane Mandelbaum, a beautiful
and brainy scholar in seventeenth-century literature with a particular
interest in the poet George Herbert. She is hired because she is not a
feminist and because, as time will reveal, she is emotionally vulnerable.
Not only is she *not* a feminist, but she is fixedly opposed to feminism,
refusing to believe that she was selected because of gender.

With Reed Amhearst somewhere in Asia or Africa for the duration of
the novel, Kate Fansler solves the puzzle alone. Joan Theresa, a radical
feminist, a lesbian in a Cambridge commune, arrives in New York to
beseech Fansler for help; Fansler agrees to accept a fellowship at Harvard
for the semester and to help Mandelbaum. Mandelbaum had been found
intoxicated in the bathtub of a women's room in Warren Hall, Harvard,
with Luellen May, a lesbian who was called to help under the pretext
that one of her "sisters" was in trouble. Mandelbaum herself asked for
Fansler's help via Joan Theresa because they were both graduate students at the same university, although they did not keep in touch in the
intervening years.

Fansler's sleuthing reveals that Howard Falkland, a graduate student,
mixed vodka with the Campari that Janet favored and conspired in what
he later called a "prank." When Janet Mandelbaum is later found dead
from cyanide in the men's room of Warren Hall, the possible miscreants
are several: Howard Falkland; Professor Allen Clarkville of the English
Department; Milton "Moon" Mandelbaum, Janet's ex-husband, from
whom she has been divorced for more than 20 years; Luellen May; and
even Kate herself. Fansler explains that cyanide, when ingested, acts
immediately in causing a painful death.

Amanda Cross, in characterizing the men and women in this novel,
uses Manichean absolutes. Moon, Andy Sladovski, professor in the
Department of English, and, of course, John Cunningham, the lawyer,
who also appeared in *The James Joyce Murder,* are feminists and good men.
Bill, Janet's brother, Howard Falkland, and Allen Clarkville are portrayed as condescendingly patriarchal and disturbed chauvinists, who,
despising intelligent women and feminists, consign them to their traditional roles of housekeeping and motherhood.

Falkland, a sycophant currying favor with Clarkville, plays a dangerous joke on Janet and then compounds the scandal by calling Luellen
May, a radical lesbian, to demean Janet further. At a dinner party,
Howard drinks too much and becomes paranoid, believing himself
trapped in a gathering of women's "libbers," the group consisting of two
men and three women. He declares, "O.K., I'm still a male chauvinist

pig. I think women are happier when they're looking up to some man and having kids, which is what nature intended them for."[3]

Allen Clarkville, also a suspect, admits to Fansler that he was unconditionally opposed to women in the English Department at Harvard. When Janet was alive, he indicted her because she was out of her depth, even though she was a recognized scholar.

In discussing Janet and women with Kate Fansler, Clarkville says that if he were given the choice, there would not be a woman in the department. "It's bound to cause problems, just in the nature of things . . . [but] then, of course, I *was* glad that Janet wasn't a real feminist" (*DTP*, 160). When he deplores women's literature courses, Kate fences with him. It is during this conversation that Kate urges Clarkville to admit that it was *he* who moved Janet's dead body from the office of the chair of the English Department to the men's room.

In her commanding way, Kate insists on hearing all of the details of the department meeting after which Janet's death occurred. Clarkville summarizes the agenda, which included possible hirings and promotions as well as a petition for some women's studies courses to be offered by the English Department. When the question came up of who would teach these women's studies courses, all men looked at Janet, who "flew off the handle," insisting that she was a scholar in the seventeenth century and did not know what the woman's point of view was in Milton, Marvell, or Donne. The coup de grâce was dealt, according to the account by Clarkville, when a member of the department huffily said, "Since it is only the efforts of those women's studies devotees who have brought you here, Professor Mandelbaum, I can't imagine why you want to take so high and mighty a tone. Of course, women's studies are nonsense, pure nonsense. So is affirmative action. . . But since we've got saddled with you, it does seem the least you could do would be to take care of this problem for us" (*DTP*, 164).

Even Clarkville was perturbed by his colleague's "terrible honesty," his tactlessness, although, ironically, he admits that the department had confirmed the search committee's choice of a woman professor who was "perfectly safe on the subject of feminism and women's studies" (*DTP*, 165). He fails to mention that there were no women on this search committee.

Kate, in her role as detective after Janet's death, offers a number of conjectures and explanations to Clarkville as to why Janet's body was moved. Among them is her suggestion that *he* must have moved Janet after her death from the chairman's office to spare him embarrassment.

He admits to moving Mandelbaum to the men's room because carrying her to the ladies' room would not be fair to the secretaries. At this point, Fansler believes that someone either forced or persuaded Janet to have a drink containing cyanide.

Apart from the portrayal of Janet Mandelbaum as a woman with masculine values—lack of empathy for women, competitiveness, and lack of sensitivity to others—she is also shown to be friendless, to take complete solace and refuge in her scholarship and to be the unhappiest of women. Readers may experience primarily negative feelings for Janet Mandelbaum.

Other women in the novel elicit from the reader several levels of understanding. Both Joan Theresa and Luellen May, radical feminists and lesbians who have completely cut off emotional ties with men, are portrayed with empathy, together with some humor, as they show little flexibility in their bias against women who do enjoy the company of men. Kate makes her own position, of course, clear, and although she accepts their view, she does not underwrite their philosophy. Kate recognizes and sympathizes with Luellen's problems, especially when Luellen's exhusband attempts to gain custody of their children, not because he loves them but because Luellen lives in a radical feminist commune. At the end of the novel, Kate agrees to help Luellen in gaining the court's approval to keep her children because she is a caring mother, although judges have been known to rule against such women.

Sylvia Farnum, a dear friend who invites Kate to share her Cambridge flat when Farnum's husband is not there, discusses with Kate many of Harvard's problems and its animosity toward women faculty. They also discuss their marriages. Sylvia's husband is often away, and it is apparent that she is not happily married. As in *The Question of Max*, Kate articulates her happiness in being married to Reed. She tells Sylvia, "Reed always knew I had to have times without him. I always knew he never bored me when I was with him. He's a male strangely composed: the pomposity was omitted. Though I miss him, I don't pine for him when we're apart, nor pine for solitude when we're together" (*DTP*, 24). What she fails to mention is the delight that she and Reed give each other in their frequent meeting of minds and witty conversations. Perhaps Kate does not wish to discomfit Sylvia with the sharp differences in their marriages.

Kate unravels the puzzle of Janet's murder through research, reading, and synthesis. In Janet's bedroom, with Janet's brother, Bill, consummate chauvinist, hovering about, Kate notices a book, *George Herbert and the Seventeenth-Century Religious Poets,* opened to the Herbert poem "Love III." She reads the poem (which the novel reprints in its entirety), asks Bill whether she might buy the book, and then gives him a check. It is astonishing that he accepts the money. During this scene, Bill is portrayed as so rigidly anti-feminist that the scene ends with, "Bill, Kate had to admit, was enough to put off sex forever" (*DTP,* 154). Later, Kate tells her lawyer/friend John Cunningham that "Love III" might be read in many ways, but that to her it seemed an invitation to death, that one is prepared to meet Christ in heaven via eating. "Eating death, perhaps."

Another clue Kate pursues is a note in the table of contents to another Herbert poem, "Hope," written in Janet's hand, next to the entry for "Love III." Kate finally locates a copy of the poem and tells Cunningham that Herbert "had had hope of returns from Hope, because he had believed in him" (*DTP,* 184), but at the poem's end, he felt abandoned, even as Janet felt, finally, that there was no return from hoping for acceptance by the solidly male contingent that was her department.

The third clue Kate uncovers is the book Janet had been reading before her death, a biography of Eleanor Marx, daughter of Karl, by Yvonne Kapp. Eleanor Marx was well known for her translation of *Madame Bovary* by Gustave Flaubert, whose heroine, in desperation at her unhappy life, commits suicide by swallowing arsenic. Ms. Marx also killed herself, but with cyanide. Simone Weil, a French philosophic writer who joined the Resistance in World War II and whose death was officially ruled a suicide (although she voluntarily underwent starvation to identify with her French compatriots), also read Herbert, as Janet was well aware. All these readings coalesce around the subject of suicide, which apparently was preying on Janet's mind. Kate also finds out from Moon that during World War II, he, like many others, was given cyanide pills to take in an emergency and that he gave some to Janet years ago. Kate concludes that Janet's swallowing the cyanide in the English chair's office was a gesture that needed no explanation; it says that Harvard's English Department virtually murdered Janet by its brutal treatment of her.

Throughout the novel, Heilbrun heaps scorn on Harvard's policies concerning women, its elitism, and its reluctance to change institutional chauvinism. Kate, through her niece Leighton Fansler, a student at Radcliffe, learns of the appeal and magic to students of even the name Harvard. Many present or prospective students feel a degree from Harvard will assure their future success. Yet, when Kate talks with those students on campus, she finds that many are considered "superficial, interested either in marks, or in sex, or in having an intense relationship, which is always so conventional they might have read about it in a book—or, well, frankly, dull and self-absorbed" (*DTP,* 96). When Kate asks what makes Harvard different, one reply was, "Almost no one is happy here" (*DTP,* 97).

Kate laments Janet's death, attributing it partly to her unrealistic expectations that the men would accept her as a member of their male club, for her scholarship, not for her gender. Kate, however, feels guilty that she failed to support Janet emotionally in the "hell she was in." Kate vows to help other women in time to come.

A theme in the book is expressed through Sylvia's cogent statement in the final chapter. "Janet was murdered all the same. . . . We all conspired in it. We isolated her, we gave her no community. Only death welcomed her" (*DTP,* 187). Women need the support of a community of women to survive.

The novel, though, ends on a note of hope: Harvard has some idea of its complicity, there will be two endowed chairs for tenured women, and Sylvia will serve on the search committee so that strong and feminist women will be chosen, ready to cope with some men who will still seek to drive them away from campus or from life.

The novel's themes concern the dangers of male power structures in a university, institutional self-glorification, differing levels of feminism, the dangers of women bonding with men at the expense of their feminism, and the irony of education failing to create a viable value system and a community of learning. Here again, Heilbrun uses literature to solve the puzzle, filling the pages with quotations that give pleasure to those readers who revel in epigrams, paradoxes, irony, and wit.

The reviewers and critics of *Death in a Tenured Position* expressed mixed feelings about the book, but most of them, while deploring the weak plot/puzzle, commended the novel for its willingness to confront the self-spawned difficulties of Harvard University.

Patricia Craig, in the *Times Literary Supplement,* writes that "this novel has neither the density of plot that distinguished *The Question of Max . . .* nor the scholarly ebullience [of] *Poetic Justice.*"[4] She compares the novel unfavorably with Dorothy Sayers's *Gaudy Night,* set in Oxford University, but Craig writes that Amanda Cross's "narrative delicacy and cogency" remain unassailed.

In *Harper's Magazine,* Jeffrey Burke comments, "Though I found the solution disappointing, I thought the solving, which depends on psychological insight and sly literary clues, top-notch."[5]

Jean M. White, in a review for the *Washington Post,* says she enjoyed the novel, claiming that Cross had "wicked fun" in attacking entrenched male power and sexism at Harvard. "Murder doesn't have to be a dreadful, dreary business. . . . It can be told in a civilized, witty, and learned fashion with an observant eye on society's pretensions and pomposities."[6]

The review by John Leonard in the *New York Times,* generally favorable, insists that Heilbrun, always quoting people in her mysteries, tries to be like Harriet Vane in a Dorothy Sayers novel. He believes this book is angry and acidulous, that the tone is bitter, and that the author aimed to revile rather than entertain. "She not only makes her point; she also hammers on it, leaving a nail in our skulls. That we, and Harvard, deserve that nail, is uncontestable."[7]

Sweet Death, Kind Death

In 1984, three years after the publication of *Death in a Tenured Position,* when Carolyn Heilbrun had reached the age of 58, her seventh mystery novel in the Amanda Cross series appeared. As we'll see, age 58 is a significant one in the novel. In *Sweet Death, Kind Death,* she departs from the themes of her other books to rivet her concerns on gender studies in college curricula, the rich possibilities for women in middle age to live adventurous lives, and death.

Haunting the novel are several women who either attempted suicide or succeeded in taking their lives. One is Stevie Smith, who wrote a poem whose penultimate line—"Sweet Death, Kind Death"—Heilbrun took for her title. Smith attempted suicide, but died of a brain tumor at age 60. Virginia Woolf, quoted at least 25 times in the novel, finally, at 59, after a series of suicide attempts, succeeded in walking into the river Ouse with rocks in her pockets. Charlotte Perkins Gilman, an American (1860–1935) who committed suicide when the ravages of cancer became intolerable to her, had been a prominent theorist of the women's movement in the United States, writing poetry, short stories, and essays of social import, her most important book being *Women and Economics.* Both Patrice Umphelby, the core character in the novel, and Kate Fansler are inspired by Gilman, who believed that women's sexual and maternal roles militated against their potential, socially and economically. True freedom for women, Gilman asserted, would come only with economic independence.

When Patrice, the only tenured professor in history at Clare College for women in New England, is found dead in the lake on the college grounds, people assume that she committed suicide. Eccentric, independent, and unafraid to take risks, she talked about her thoughts on God and death. "One should not wait around to be invaded by old age," said Patrice[8]. Years earlier, Kate Fansler, meeting Patrice briefly at a fog-bound airport in Scotland, produced a flask filled with Laphroaig, a single Islay malt Scotch, the Gaelic word *laphroaig* meaning, "The beautiful hollow by the broad bay." The two drank the Laphroaig, with its earthy, peaty flavor, and talked about the existence of God. Kate, when asked by Patrice about the existence of God, said that she thought "belief in God was a comfort to those who could not contemplate the unfairness of life without such melioration" (*SD*, 5). Fansler then quoted Mrs. Ramsey in Virginia Woolf's *To the Lighthouse,* who questioned how any superior being could create this world lacking reason, order, and justice, where suffering, death, and poverty were everywhere, and where there was no evil too ignoble for humans to commit. Patrice flatly stated that God did not exist. Although this meeting was the only one between these two women, Patrice had intrigued Kate Fansler, who nonetheless did not recall the episode at the airport until Herbert and Archer, two men writing Patrice Umphelby's biography, approached her.

Throughout the book the personality and character of Patrice Umphelby are fleshed out by Archer, who knew her; by two segments of her journals; by colleagues from Clare College; and by one of her two children. From Patrice's journal, given by Herbert and Archer to Kate, she learns Patrice's ideas about biography for women (their looking back instead of ahead), and she, too, quotes Virginia Woolf's idea of moments of intensity. Patrice faces the reality that she is old, but this reality does not depress her; it fills her with joy. "I have fallen in love with death, and love, if one does not pursue the object incontinently, is joyous" (*SD*, 28). She hopes, when the proper time arrives, to urge sweet death to come to her. At one time, Patrice recognized that impending death gave intensity to middle age, even as youth's intensity came from passion and hope. Despite Patrice's ideas about death, Archer and Herbert believe that she was murdered.

Kate then receives a telephone call from President Norton of Clare College, who proposes that Kate put questions about Patrice's death to rest by coming to the college under the "cover" of an appointment to the task force on gender studies. Kate accepts immediately. President Norton is a conservative, a lawyer, a woman who is unconvinced that gender studies is a viable option, but she has formed the task force to discuss the possibility. Norton feels Patrice was a gadfly who created trouble on the campus and who even in death would be a problem. "Death was clearly the damn woman's favorite subject" (*SD*, 47).

At a cocktail party, Kate finds the college faculty to be almost wholly conservative, to be opposed to gender studies, and to have disliked Patrice, an eccentric who wrote witty short stories and novels, such as *The Years of the Red Cat,* published her stories in the *New Yorker,* and gave seminars around the country. Her specialty was history between the world wars. A classics professor at the party told Kate that he thought Antigone was a pig-headed fool. Only a few faculty respected and admired Patrice; Kate felt any of them might have killed her. One of Patrice's admirers told Kate that during the struggle in Congress to pass the Equal Rights Amendment, not one northeast women's college testified in its favor.

A friend of Patrice, Veronica Manfred, refuses to believe Patrice committed suicide because the suicide note was addressed only to her children and not also to her, a dear friend. The note was typed, a duplicate of Charlotte Perkins Gilman's final note, which talks about ending one's life only when some power to serve people is gone, and then finding a way for death to be quick and easy. Veronica insists that anyone might have typed the note, that Patrice would have found her own words for a note like this, and that the person who typed it knew about Patrice's admiration for Gilman.

Visiting Patrice's daughter, Dr. Sarah Umphelby, Kate learns that her mother had had cancer, like Gilman, and for a while it seemed that Patrice did commit suicide. But Sarah had recently found the last part of Patrice's journal, and it is a panegyric for adventure. Patrice quotes the Roman general Pompey's address to his crew, "'*Navigare necesse est vivere non necesse,*'" meaning, "It is necessary to sail; it is not necessary to live" (*SD*, 112). This famous quotation suggests that it is essential to be free to sail, to explore, to find adventure, to be concerned not with living per se but with the content of that living. Patrice discusses the inevitability of death. She believes people must consider death as part of their future and should not hold onto the past. The journal also alludes to Virginia Woolf's passionate, compulsive desire at age 56 to write a particular book. As the journal ends, Patrice worries about the survival of Clare College, given the general fearfulness of the women on its faculty, and smites the classics prig of a professor who feels that Greek literature could be in danger of betrayal by modern interpretations.

Having finished reading Patrice's journal, Kate feels a deep kinship with her. "Perhaps she asked me about God, not because she hoped to believe, but because she wondered if she was alone in her terrible disbelief in the sanctity of the past" (*SD,* 113–14).

This extended summary reveals additional themes in the novel: that the young are taught by opinionated, conservative, narrow-minded men and women who refuse to accept change, that they envy professors like Patrice, whose obvious aim was to agitate and stimulate students and teachers to become more flexible and to modernize. Still another theme is that the nearing of death need not be a horror for the middle-aged: every moment in middle age becomes more precious and living intensely can be a joy. Some people, like Gilman, place priority on the service to others.

The two most important characters are, of course, Kate Fansler and Patrice, who, already dead, is brought to life by the many who knew her, even by the professors who felt threatened by the volcanic force of her independence and her iconoclasm. Like Socrates, in a sense, she threatened the status quo, startled the mediocre, and had to be silenced.

Fansler, with some input from Herbert and Archer, solves the mystery puzzle. Why would Patrice, who alludes to Virginia Woolf's passion to write a book when she was near Patrice's age, take her life while at work on her own book? Kate talks to countless faculty members about Patrice, attends dinners, spends hours dissecting details with Herbert and Archer, and finally solves the puzzle: a faculty member and his wife did indeed murder Patrice.

Archer and Herbert delight Kate Fansler, who during their many meetings introduces them to the costly beverage from Islay. Their insight, their sensitivity to women, their wit and perspicacity endear them to Kate, who uses their collaborative research in her sleuthing. Archer is universally admired and more intuitive than Herbert, who is more organized and serious. Archer says of Patrice, "She was madly eccentric by any normal womanly standards, and wholly delightful, which is, my dear, a rare combination" (*SD,* 7). He went so far as virtually to canonize Patrice as saint.

In *Sweet Death, Kind Death,* Reed surprises Kate by arranging to leave his job in the attorney general's office to teach criminal procedure at the Columbia University Law School, telling Kate, "There comes a moment . . . when one has to move forward, when it is impossible to stay in the same place without moving back" (*SW,* 22–23). A continual threnody in the marriage of Kate and Reed is their conversational parry and thrust to observe the principle of leaving each other space. Kate marvels about her marriage to Reed: "How can I be this fortunate? How is it possible? And what will the gods say if they hear me?" (*SD,* 82).

In *Sweet Death, Kind Death,* Reed Amhearst has almost no direct role in solving the puzzle, and since Kate splits her time between Boston and New York and between Reed and Clare College, it is evident that he is not in some Third World country on research or aiding with police investigation. He stands in marked contrast to virtually all of the male faculty at Clare; he is flexible, kind, expansive, and a feminist; they narcissistic, desiccated, fearful of change, and male chauvinists.

Despite opposition by most Clare faculty (especially by Professor Fiorelli, who thought teaching in an all-women's college with gender studies would turn him into a eunuch and who equated gender studies with lesbian interests), the task force recommended that gender studies be integrated into the curriculum. President Norton agrees to follow the decision of the committee—at least for a time.

Another motif in the book is the questioning of the rationale for the continuance of all-women's colleges and their ultimate survival. The link that connects gender studies with the viability of women's institutions is made by Lucy, a faculty wife, whose husband admired Patrice. She tells Kate, "In a women's college, you are careful not to seem to be questioning the family, the place of women, old views of God" (*SD,* 126).

Among rational, flexible, and imaginative men and women, Cross seems to be saying, Patrice becomes a symbol of professor par excellence, teaching her young students to think and to develop sound values in a changing world. For women, particularly those who fear growing old or useless, after their children have grown and left, Patrice becomes a model for turning middle age into the best years of their lives.

Critical comments on *Sweet Death, Kind Death,* differ, ranging from condemnation to praise. Perhaps the most negative, even perverse comment appeared in the *New Yorker,* in an unsigned short article in the "Mystery and Crime" column. The book is dismissed as a "lamebrained mystery," the writer believing that "Kate's taste for gin and cigarettes seems intended to make her appear decadent," but the reviewer believes the dialogue between Kate and Reed "compares favorably with that of Myrna Loy and William Powell" in the *Thin Man* series.[9]

In the *London Times Literary Supplement,* T. J. Bunyan calls *Sweet Death, Kind Death,* "A cool, elegant and erudite book, full of apposite quotations, with a great deal of witty, if mannered conversation, all washed down on a flood-tide of gin and Laphroaig." The writer's caveat is that "action and detection are at the bottom of the list of ingredients."[10]

Newgate Callendar of the *New York Times Book Review* had mixed reactions to the book. "The writing is full of literary allusions, cultural mur-

murings and polite civilities. But the dialogue does not ring true. Perhaps the Amanda Cross books are an acquired taste; certainly she has her circle of admirers. . . . Nearly everybody speaks so elegantly and genteelly that it suggests tea drinking with pinkie extended."[11]

None of the three commentators addresses the social vision of gender studies, the question of the need for women's colleges, or the crisis of middle age for women who have had "to buy into the dream of youth" (*SD,* 127).

No Word from Winifred

Amanda Cross's eighth novel, *No Word from Winifred,* published in 1986, two years after the appearance of *Sweet Death, Kind Death,* is a mystery, but not a murder mystery novel. The protagonist, Winifred Ashby, simply vanishes and is found to be alive at the end of the story. Kate Fansler never meets Winifred, yet by the novel's end, as she pieces together a multitude of details concerning the missing woman from various sources, Kate says, "I love Winifred. . . . I think she was a remarkable, a wonderful person."[12]

The novel's puzzle revolves around Winifred, honorary niece of Charlotte Stanton, once a tutor and later a principal of an Oxford college, and famous author of popular fiction about ancient Greece. For a number of summers, beginning when Winifred was eight years old, Charlotte invited her to stay at Oxford, where she would room with the family from whom Charlotte rented her apartment. These summers became Edenic for Winifred, her remembrances recalling for some readers Wordsworth's "splendor in the grass" or Charles Ryder's delirium at Brideshead with Sebastian in *Brideshead Revisited*—idyllic and romantic, joyous and carefree.

No Word from Winifred develops in a nonlinear pattern. The story is told through flashbacks: Winifred's journal of 40 pages; letters from Charlotte Lucas, who worked from time to time in the law firm employing Fansler's niece, Leighton, and who wishes to write a biography of Stanton; reports from an investigator, from friends and acquaintances of Winifred, and from Leighton; and myriad interviews conducted by Kate Fansler. Aunt Stanton promises to help Winifred if in years to come she is accepted by Oxford University, but this plan never becomes reality. Before Winifred's recollections of the city of Oxford, she writes in her journal of being employed part of the day on a Massachusetts farm owned by Ted and Jean Wilkowski, milking cows for a small sum plus free housing. This arrangement gives her a small income and helps to structure her day, which includes writing. In her journal, Winifred writes, "What marks a writer is this: until she—or he, of course—writes down whatever happened, turns it into a story, it hasn't really happened, it hasn't shape, form, reality. I think so many women keep diaries and journals in the hope of giving some shape to their inchoate lives" (*NWW*, 35).

Winifred's journal resonates with a number of perceptions, thoughts, and wishes—her Cartesian predilection for routine, reflections on books read (by Joseph Campbell, Suzanne Langer, Georges Simenon), privacy and solitude, hatred of civilization, and a love of nature, albeit "full of pain and fear for its demise" (*NWW*, 39).

During the course of her several summers at Oxford, Winifred became close friends with Cyril, the owner's son. One of the reasons they became fast friends was that she was a girl and thus no threat to him. One summer, Winifred noticed Cyril's mother weeping. Winifred's reaction reveals an unsparing intelligence and a sharp insight, especially for one so young. "The terrible pity and scorn I felt for her (not, notice, terror; it never occurred to me that I could end up like her, and I did not) are palpable to me still," she wrote (*NWW*, 51). Cyril's father, an Oxford don, dined every evening in college hall, a routine causing his wife severe loneliness. Winifred scorned her for being a fool and exonerated her husband for thinking his wife a bore. The first section of the journal ends with the telling thought: "But for me England is always that first year, when I was not unalterably committed to a girl's destiny, and had found [Cyril]" (*NWW*, 59).

Living with her father and stepmother in America, Winifred never knew her real mother, but comments in her journal that she has no need to find her, that women, after the so-called romantic days of early marriage, having so little adventure in their lives, look backward instead of anticipating and creating future adventures. "This backward search," she writes, "which makes good novels, makes bad living" (*NWW*, 63). Winifred yearned to create her own present time.

Creating her own destiny *now*, Winifred develops much rapport with her farmer employers and revels in her privacy and solitude. She knows it will end, as it does when Charlotte Lucas ("Charlie"), a friend of Toby Van Dine, a law partner of Kate's brother, sends Winifred a letter asking for a meeting. Meeting with Charlie, who wishes to write a biography of Charlotte Stanton, Winifred receives a letter from Harriet St. John Merriweather ("Sinjin"), a friend of Stanton, now deceased, asking her to come to England, all expenses paid, before she makes her will. Winifred agrees to go. Sinjin, about eighty years of age, is a specialist on Tudor times; having met her, Winifred likes and admires her, since Sinjin, like Stanton, feels, "'It's the work you do that matters'" (*NWW*, 81). Agreeing to leave control of the Stanton papers to Winifred, Sinjin agrees with Winifred that Charlie will be a suitable biographer. The elder woman also arranges to have her son and Winifred share proceeds from Stanton's books. In a letter to Toby, Charlie notes that she doesn't know why, but to Winifred, "Sinjin is some sort of miracle dropped into Winifred's path" (*NWW*, 85). Only at the end of the novel does Kate conclude that Sinjin is Winifred's mother.

Shortly after her last meeting with Sinjin, Winifred disappears, and for the remaining two-thirds of the book, Kate, Charlie, a private detective, and Leighton band together and attempt to unravel the mystery of her disappearance. It is Kate's sleuthing that leads her to the office of the Modern Language Association headquarters, an MLA convention in New York City, and a meeting there with three professors, all of whom help Kate to gather crucial details on the life of Winifred Ashby.

Winifred's relationship with men never comes up in her journal, Charlie's letters, or any report. Details concerning Winifred's love affair with Martin Heffenreffer, a married professor, surface when his wife, Mary Louise ("Biddy"), tells Kate. Although the Heffenreffers are estranged, they still occupy the same house. Curiously, Biddy and Winifred meet and begin to admire each other unconditionally, and when she realizes Biddy is married to Martin, Winifred tells her of their affair. Biddy is not at all distressed; Martin, however, by chance encountering the two laughing in a restaurant and aware of their closeness, explodes at, as he terms it, their "betrayal." Winifred has no interest in marriage; she wants only a part-time man. Kate approves of this preference but speaks of "the shift from a male-centered life to a life where love for men was still possible but not exclusive" (*NWW*, 194). Then Kate comments on a theme that appears in several of the Cross novels and in Heilbrun's books on feminism, that deep-rooted friendships between women are rarely written about.

Cross often speaks of quests that men pursue, while women remain inactive. In this novel, conversely, the women pursue adventures: Kate wants to solve the puzzle, Leighton to become Watson to Kate's Holmes, and Charlie to become Stanton's biographer. Of course, above all, there is Winifred's quest to control her own destiny completely. All of these questing women become, in a sense, feminine versions of Ulysses, while the men, left behind with their mundane problems, become Penelopes. All of this results in role reversals, to be sure.

Although both Kate and Reed are highly intelligent and intuitive, sharp-witted and imaginative, they arrive at an astonishingly wrong conclusion—that Martin killed Winifred and buried her body in the basement of the house that he left to Biddy. The most amusing scene in the book takes place in the Fansler-Amhearst flat when Reed, worried that Martin may be dangerous, hides in an adjacent room with a detective while Kate attempts to extract details of Winifred's supposed burial from Martin.

Confronted with Kate's question, Martin, apoplectic, denies killing Winifred, but admits that he was obsessed with her and at one point did want to kill her. Martin tells Kate that he found out that he was useful to both Winifred and Biddy. "That Winifred loved me, but loved Biddy too; Biddy loved me, but loved Winifred. Can you imagine what that was like?" (*NWW*, 246). And because of Martin's obsessive love for Winifred, he exacts her promise to leave America and Europe forever, to go where he could not find her. Winifred tells Martin that she will go to India, at least for a while. Although some readers may see manipulation of Winifred by Martin in this arrangement, Kate says that Winifred is at heart a wanderer, that she could never be exiled, that her "gift for friendship and for solitude, is an excellent combination" (*NWW*, 255).

Kate portrays Winifred at a narrative distance, never having met her, as a role model of feminism, completely independent. Some readers, though, may perceive Winifred as a role model of solipsism: she is the very center of her universe. Unlike the admirable Charlotte Perkins Gilman (mentioned in *Sweet Death, Kind Death*), who used her energy to the last erg in service to others, Winifred gives her solitude top priority and deserts not only her two farmer employers but Biddy as well.

No Word from Winifred is distinct from all of Cross's earlier novels in using no epigraphs and almost no literary quotes, although literary allusions are liberally scattered throughout the book. The novel is structured around narratives at several removes (*vide* journals, letters, reports) and with not a scintilla of suspense; the dialogue lacks sprightliness, though some humor stems from Leighton's role as Watson to Kate's Sherlock Holmes. Despite its flaws, the novel is affecting in its motifs—that male superiority still controls the power structure, that the need for psychic and economic independence for women is crucial, that most marriages bind women as codependents and constrict their need for self-development, and that questing women fulfill themselves in becoming more lively and exciting companions to both women and men.

No Word from Winifred receives high praise from Rebecca R. Butler. She writes: "This is a feminist book that transcends the stereotypical. Both the women and the men whom Kate encounters along the trail of clues are believable individuals, as recognizable as Geoffrey Chaucer's pilgrims must have been to literate Londoners at the close of the fourteenth century." She also writes, "Thanks to Kate Fansler, her frivolous air and her sincere heart and her literary mind, the American detective story has achieved charm, spirit, and wit" (429–30).

A Trap for Fools

The title of this novel is taken from Rudyard Kipling's "If": "If you can bear to hear the truth you've spoken / Twisted by knaves to make a trap for fools . . ." Each chapter of the novel uses as an epigraph two or four lines from the poem, and each segment of the poem is integrated into action, character, or theme.

A Trap for Fools, the ninth in the Kate Fansler mystery series, published in 1989, three years after *No Word from Winifred,* emerges as a more engaging novel than its predecessor, wherein no murder was committed. Because the novel starts with an act of murder that creates chaos in the academic community, there is movement, shaped by confrontational and humorous dialogue, together with an array of well-contoured characters and ideas that embrace feminism and the black community in the kind of campus setting Amanda Cross knows best.

The first sentence of the novel reads: "The body was found early on Sunday morning by a member of the university security force patrolling the campus."[13] The victim is Professor Canfield Adams ("Canny"), a scholar in Islamic studies, and so vehement and widespread was the hatred for him that any number of faculty members, administrators, or students might have pushed him out of his seventh-floor office window on Thanksgiving weekend. Petulance, pomposity, narcissism, manipulation, and sexism characterized Canny, whom the author describes as "defenestrated." Since there appeared to have been foul play, the provost, aware of Kate's background in crime solving, called on her to help, promising all the resources of the university. Kate, deeply resistant to accepting the assignment, is urged on by her friend Edna Hoskins, dean of the professional schools, who tells Kate she has "remarkable lucidity of intellect." Later, she reminds Kate that she has agreed to help "To keep the police from making dreadful mischief, to keep from stoking the fires of racism, which are already smoldering in this city and probably in this university, and to discover the truth or a reasonable facsimile thereof" (*TF*, 56). Especially insistent in persuading Kate to investigate the murder is Matthew Noble, vice president for internal affairs at the university.

Kate tells Reed that the university's asking her to solve the mystery is a trick; she thinks those involved hope she will fail and make a fool of herself. Eventually, however, she agrees to help solve the case because her friend Humphrey Edgerton, a black professor of American and African-American literature, has no alibi and is under suspicion.

In her thoroughgoing and vigorous way, Kate talks to a parade of people who might be involved: Butler, a security guard, quick-witted, anti-feminist, who despite his knowledge of Kate's feminism agrees to help her; Cecilia Adams, wife of the deceased, materialistic, narcissistic, and an alcoholic, whom Kate rather likes for her "refreshing openness, the more valued in a university community, where egoism was disguised as scholarly rigor and enjoyment as intellectual despair" (*TF*, 44); Penelope Constable, English novelist, who, surprisingly, had a brief affair with the universally disliked Adams, who could be charming as he wished; Gabriel Witherspoon, a retired wealthy benefactor and donor to the university and an appreciative exstudent of Adams; Peter Pettipas, Harvard University Press editor; Arabella Jordan, a black student, feisty and enraged at the world, who says, "It's no picnic being black in this lily-white mausoleum" (*TF*, 122); and Dr. Clemance Anthony, wife of one of Adams's son, an authoritative Freudian psychoanalyst, who castigates Cecilia Adams as being wholly without ego. "She is the strongest argument I know to substantiate Freud's view of the lack of moral development in women" (*TF*, 170). Kate spars with Dr. Anthony and holds her own in an amusing dialogue. Kate also interviews secretaries, who virtually run the departments and know all the gossip, and city police, who condescendingly cooperate with her. All of these characterizations are deft. In *A Trap for Fools*, Heilbrun has perhaps for the first time in the Cross novels shaped men and women with enough individuality and charisma for the reader to recall them easily, especially Arabella, Humphrey and Gabriel, and Butler.

As the weeks pass by and Kate makes absolutely no progress, she suffers frustration, which turns into anger and self-reproach when Arabella Jordan is murdered in the same way that Adams was—by being pushed out of a window. Kate is devastated by guilt from having interviewed

Arabella and, as she thinks, giving cause for the student's murder. Her despair is so keen that Reed returns from Amsterdam, where he had gone to a conference, to console Kate, who has an obsessional need to talk. When she apologizes to Reed for having to bear the brunt of her despondency, he tells her repeatedly that that "was what he was there for" (*TF,* 138).

Through some cognitive, intuitive process, Kate winnows out the innocent. When she articulates her thoughts to Reed, he notes that good investigators, criminal or scholarly, need to make a sudden leap, but he adds, "In the end, it comes together in your mind or not at all. That's true of detective work, biography, history, even science" (*TF,* 193).

When Kate encounters Matthew Noble, the murderer, who threatens her near the campus, she already knows that he has used her as a diversion to escape being identified as the killer; in initiating the campus investigation he took pressure off the city police. Kate has already determined the motive for the two murders: Noble's siphoning money from a huge grant for Islamic studies. When Adams discovered the embezzlement and threatened to reveal Noble, he was killed. Arabella, too, found out, and so was also killed. Arabella had for a time presumably put pressure on Noble to create scholarships for black students or a black professorship.

Unlike many detective novels, this one gives no hint of the murderer's identity; nor is there a clue concerning the perfidy of Edna Hoskins, who had also discovered Noble's fund skimming but kept silent while accepting money from the vice president. In a highly dramatic scene, Kate confronts Edna with her hypocrisy for having used her friendship with Kate to influence her to undertake the investigation. Impassioned, Kate says to Edna, "You led me on with a little charade of deception that would make John le Carré's characters look like folks from a nursery rhyme" (*TF,* 205). This scene is one of the best in the novel, exclaiming the reality of rank betrayal. Edna admits that Kate was a "diversion" but that she was forced into collusion with Noble and felt too weak to unmask him. Noble, says Kate, like many others, underestimated the anger of people who appear powerless, and he also failed to perceive Kate's tendency to look for narratives. "That's my profession, not being a detective. That's the profession of every professor of literature. He thought to provide a diversion, but lit crit teaches you to be on the watchout for exactly that. We deal in subtexts, in the hidden story" (*TF,* 210). This quote of course underscores the value of literature in detection—whether in the humanities or in homicide.

When Kate identifies the murderer to the provost, who is shocked, she uses the leverage of "good" blackmail. She will spare the university the embarrassment of having all the facts of the case made public if the provost agrees to fund three scholarships in the name of Arabella Jordan, preferably for "shes," but Kate does not want to be sexist, she says. When the provost thinks Kate might settle for one or two, Kate retorts, "Three. It's a holy number" (*TF,* 213).

A Trap for Fools covers some new terrain for Heilbrun in its exploration of the compelling problems African Americans face in academia, the difficulty of friendships between black and white women, the thinly veiled racism of the police and other sources of security, and the end of friendship through betrayal. Beyond such themes, the author continues to present her ideas through the prism of feminism.

An interesting critical comment on this book is made by Maureen T. Reddy, who was disturbed by the ending, "with Kate using the tactics of the oppressors to obtain reparations for the oppressed." When she tells the provost that she learned something about blackmail, she then blackmails him for the scholarships in return for her cooperation in keeping the embezzlement out of the press. "Through exerting this illegitimate form of power," says Reddy, "Kate loses her legitimate power. In the final chapter, Kate ceases to speak and to act with feminist authority, abandoning a feminist standpoint and operating instead within the system of power the novel has shown to be corrupt.[14]

The Players Come Again

In 1990, a year following *A Trap for Fools,* Amanda Cross's tenth novel, *The Players Come Again,* was published, its title taken from a line in the novel *The Waves* by Virginia Woolf. It is Cross's second novel in which there is no murder, with Kate Fansler as "detective" subservient, in a way, to Kate Fansler as literary scholar and feminist, although a character in the book says, "Aren't all scholars really detectives?"[15]

The center of interest begins when Kate is asked by a highly respectable publisher to write a biography of Gabrielle Foxx, wife of Emmanuel, a famous writer whose novel *Ariadne* had been judged a masterpiece. The heroine is a lesbian who refuses to accept any role society wants to assign her. Questioning whether a male could have captured a woman's sensibility so well, some believed that Gabrielle wrote the novel.

Kate is uninterested in writing the biography until she reads the manuscript the publisher has given her of a memoir of 53 pages by Anne

Gringold, wherein the idyllic childhood of three friends is recalled. Besides Anne there is Dorinda Goddard, a girl from an enormously wealthy Jewish family, and Nellie Foxx, the supposed granddaughter of Emmanuel and Gabrielle, daughter of their son Emile and his wife, Hilda. Dorinda, the ringleader of the trio, all about 12 years of age at the beginning of their friendship, becomes fond of Anne, daughter of a widowed charwoman. Urged by Dorinda, the affluent Goddards lavish luxury on Anne (vacations on the Jersey shore, clothes, jewelry, and even a scholarship). Anne characterizes Dorinda as a moving force, adventurous and longing to conquer new worlds and presenting to Anne not only material things but also loyalty, enthusiasm, and her "aching affection." She orders Anne to accompany her everywhere—to the beach club, the riding stables and the tennis court. The three musketeers read and adore Elizabeth Bowen, the English writer of *The Death of the Heart* (1938), discuss sex and their classmates, and attend dances, all at the urging of the forthright Dorinda.

The memoir speaks of the anti-Semitism endured by the Goddards and other Jews, who, excluded from social clubs, founded their own— the Harmonie Club—for wealthy Jews from Germany and then barred membership to Eastern Europeans. Several narratives in the memoir echo Carolyn Heilbrun's experiences with anti-Semitism as related in her earlier nonfiction writings. Those days before the girls became women were paradisiacal, a magic time, and Anne writes, "I was consciously happy as part of the trio, and considered myself blessed" (*PCA*, 42).

When "time's winged chariot" arrives, as Andrew Marvell writes, all three women go their separate ways. Who could have imagined giddy and independent Dorinda, after sexual flings and impassioned living, reverting to a conventional destiny by marrying a dull surgeon and having children? Anne writes that in her generation a woman pursued marriage as if it were the Golden Fleece (*PCA*, 69). She, however, thought of marriage as a trap. Nellie, clever with languages, returns to Europe and works for an international bank, while Anne is employed in the business end of publishing. What brings these three women together again is Gabrielle, living in London, whom Anne, bound for London anyway, is asked to visit by Eleanor, Dorinda's mother. At their very first meeting, both women feel a kinship, and the next day, when Anne visits again, Gabrielle, feeling ill, begs her visitor to take all of her papers away with her *immediately*. Anne takes the papers, filling two huge sacks, and stores them in a London bank vault. Subsequently, Gabrielle is hospitalized, put in a nursing home (paid for by the Goddards), and dies some years later.

So compelling is Anne's memoir that Kate agrees to take leave from her university for a year to write the biography of Gabrielle Foxx, who had always been in the shadow of her famous husband.

In the ensuing weeks, Kate meets Dorinda, who charms her and talks about Gabrielle, and then flies to Switzerland to meet Nellie, who fills in the portrait of Gabrielle. Nellie trusts Kate sufficiently to startle her with news that she is in fact the daughter not of Hilda and Emile but of Hilda and her supposed grandfather. In effect, Nellie is Emile's half-sister, but Hilda Foxx pretended that Emile was the father. Eventually, Emile over a long period poisons his father, but if he were ever to be accused, Gabrielle would swear that *she* had killed her husband. Kate is sworn to secrecy about these Gothic details. Back home, Kate meets Anne, with whom she eventually goes to London to examine the bundles of Gabrielle's papers. Another revelation entrusted to Kate is that Anne is the daughter of Sig Goddard, Dorinda's father, and is therefore half-Jewish. Anne's mother permitted the Goddards to provide Anne with their largesse because Sig owed her, but she refused any help for herself.

Throughout Kate's association with the trio of women, she feels somewhat manipulated, and at last the truth emerges: the three did not want her to write a biography of Gabrielle but a biographical introduction to Gabrielle's novel, which they also wanted Kate to edit. Gabrielle's novel is another version of Emmanuel's novel, presented through a *woman's* sensibility.

Part of the difficulty of this Amanda Cross novel is its overreliance on narrative and its imposition of ideas on the reader—telling instead of showing. The reader has no idea beyond a surface one of the content of either Emmanuel's or Gabrielle's novel and is expected to agree to a willing suspension of disbelief. The convoluted storyline of the novel may remind some readers of John le Carré, who is quoted in this novel as well as in *A Trap of Fools* and who is a constant presence in the eleventh Kate Fansler novel, *An Imperfect Spy*.

Despite the disappointing lack of action and suspense in the storyline, the novel's motif of feminism is compelling. The friendship of women is a recurring theme in the books of Carolyn Heilbrun and Amanda Cross. Dorinda, declaring that her girlhood was the best part, says, "That for women, there is a time before the need to impress men when women can find a life with each other, a friendship, a companionship" (*PCA*, 171). These three formed close ties in girlhood and, after a gap in time, when they were in their 60s, resumed the magic circle of friendship. Kate calls them a beneficent "coven of good witches," who, no longer young, are youthful in attitude, manner, and vigor, sustained by their friendship.

Marriage is disappointment and confinement, Heilbrun implies, with men demanding that their wives satisfy their narcissistic needs while being clueless as to their wives' sensibilities. Gabrielle's marriage was a blight. Hilda went mad and went to the United States while her husband went off to France during World War II and married a Frenchwoman, only to die shortly thereafter. Eleanor's marriage seems unfulfilled because she never became aware of her own needs while her husband lived. Dorinda is in the process of getting a divorce. Nellie is happily married (as is Kate), and Anne is not married but lives with her first love in harmony.

Heilbrun uses the myth of Ariadne and Theseus in the storyline of the novel and also as one of her significant motifs—the Minoan civilization, a matriarchy, was peaceful, with men and women active as equals. She asserts that their culture represented "a civilized refinement that has not been often equalled since" (PCA, 190). The Greeks subsequently changed Crete into a patriarchal culture, which demoted the position and respect of women. Gabrielle's novel asserts that Greece admired the brutality and cruelty of men, who were sent to find in war their rewards in rape, carnage, and destruction of conquered lands. Theseus, initially aided by Ariadne, who provided the thread that enabled him to find his way out of the labyrinth, led the Greek forces in the destruction of Cretan culture.

This Cross novel also urges women not to be trapped in the past. Idyllic as was their prelapsarian Eden, Anne, Dorinda, and Nellie refuse to look back except to put time past into perspective and anticipate the future of becoming.

The most adventurous of the girls, Dorinda, forfeits her birthright of freedom and choice in marriage, but at the novel's end, she extricates herself from her failed marriage. All three women, married or not, refusing inactivity and passivity, have meaningful jobs and are not defined by men.

Of the three, Anne seems to have had the most control over her life. At Dorinda's wedding at the Harmonie Club, she reveals her modus operandi: "I could never follow a man in dancing; I always wanted to move faster, to go at my own pace" (PCA, 56). She never marries, but she does have meaningful relationships and enjoy movement at her own pace.

Those readers who know other Amanda Cross novels will notice in *The Players Come Again* the absence of epigraphs, considered a hallmark of the Kate Fansler series. The meaning of the book's title, *The Players Come Again,* as suggested by its original source, Virginia Woolf, is elusive, but Woolf seems to suggest that after we undergo a luminous epiphany, we understand not only the cycle of suffering and death but also the regeneration that follows, when another group of players appear on the earth once more, just as Anne, Dorinda, and Nellie begin their individual and collective journeys of renewal.

This novel is Amanda Cross's most intense collective portrait of the seemingly limitless possibilities open to women who sculpt their own lives. In a sense, this book is a correlate to her most popular recent non-fiction book, *Writing a Woman's Life,* discussed in the next chapter.

An Imperfect Spy

Five years following the publication of *The Players Come Again,* in 1995, the eleventh novel in the Kate Fansler series appeared. Entitled *An Imperfect Spy,* this novel resumes the use of the flagship epigraphs at the beginning of each chapter, this time from the novels of John le Carré.

The novel centers around Kate Fansler's team teaching of a course titled "Women in Law and Literature" with Blair Whitson at Schuyler Law School, a mediocre institution in New York City. Kate's husband, Reed Amhearst, also on leave from his university, joins the faculty of Schuyler primarily to establish a student-staffed legal clinic. Neither the course Kate will teach nor the legal clinic has ever been offered to the school's law students.

The all-male faculty of Schuyler Law School is antediluvian, its professors mediocre (although some have degrees from Harvard and Yale), ultraconservative, rigid, sexist, and smug in their entrenchment; the one exception is Blair Whitson, who yearns to improve the college and begins to set in motion the radical changes that will lead to a revolution. Before the arrival of Kate and Reed, he had had an ally in Nellie Rosenbusch, the only female professor at the school; she was hit and killed by a truck, and many people think it was not an accident but murder. Another supporter—still very much alive—is Harriet Furst, who had been a professor but is now head of the secretarial pool, highly efficient and well-read, who constantly quotes from the novels of John le Carré. She says, "I'm like Smiley. I have a trained, observant mind. I notice things. I have his guarded, watchful way of looking at the world."[16]

Most of the students are older, half are women, and many are minorities, some of whom wanted Professor Rosenbusch to be replaced by another woman, course offerings on women and law, and other significant changes. Blair says of the faculty, "They are beginning to smell the danger of new ideas and are rallying the troops" (*IS*, 54).

Blair and Kate design a course to include legal texts to be discussed in conjunction with literary texts such as Susan Glaspell's "A Jury of Her Peers," Thomas Hardy's *Tess of the D'Urbevilles*, and Charlotte Brontë's *Jane Eyre*. Reed's law clinic will focus on prisons, helping poor inmates who without student aid would have no chance whatsoever for legal help. One of the women desperately needing help is Betty Osborne, in prison for murdering her husband, who had been a batterer and a professor at Schuyler. She insists that the faculty perjured themselves at her trial, that evidence was withheld by the Schuyler attorneys, and that Betty's lawyer was not aware of the "battered woman's syndrome."

The "Women in Law and Literature" course starts well, but problems soon erupt: the class is literally locked in by a mischief-maker; one student, who wrongfully recorded the class lectures, begins a fistfight with Blair; and Kate is insulted by male chauvinists in and out of class and is mocked on campus. Eventually, though, some women begin to respond positively. The faculty, benighted and resistant to change, of course, become enraged at both the special class and the clinic.

Kate, assuming the role of sleuth, visits the brother of Nellie Rosenbusch in New Hampshire to collect facts about her possible murder. She questions Charles ("Rosie") Rosenbusch about faculty attitudes toward Nellie, any fear she may have had for her safety, and any enemy who would have wanted to kill her. Rosie reveals that his sister was not murdered; rather, she suffered from an illness that caused her to faint, and this had caused her death. He later offers Schuyler a monetary prize for the best law review essay on law and gender in his sister's name.

The indignant faculty attribute the wave of student discontent to Kate and Reed, convenient scapegoats. The dean sends the faculty a memorandum stating that the couple will not be invited back to Schuyler, that neither the clinic nor the course in literature in law would be offered again, and that the Rosenbusch prize offered to the school would not be accepted.

One student immediately protests the dean's pronouncements and asks who among his classmates agrees with him. In response, "The rafters shook with all the *ayes* sounded" (*IS*, 199). To nip the protest in the bud, the administration disconnects the microphones and turns off the lights. Blair, when approached by the students for help, suggests letting the publicity achieve its results; if not, he would meet with them.

All promises to end well: the court agrees to reopen Betty Osborne's case, the students are galvanized into action, and Rosie begins to recover from his grief over his sister's death. Kate and Reed *did* help to initiate many changes.

The motifs in the novel spring up like wildflowers. Kate, immersed her entire life in literature, insists that literature matters. In prison, Betty Osborne, who had been a student of Kate, asks to see her and talks at length about Thomas Hardy's Tess, who did not have the second chance that Betty has been offered. She recalls for Kate a class discussion on *Tess of the D'Urbevilles* in which it was said that Tess only *seems* "to be a victim . . . because she does something about her life. She refuses just to be passive" (*IS*, 189). Like the Hardy heroine, Betty decides to be active and to take a hand in her destiny.

The prison encounters shared by Betty, Kate, and Reed provide for the fusion of practical law and literature, as did Kate's class. The classroom sessions in literature and law, stimulating the critical thinking so crucial to students of law, also updated their knowledge of the position of women in statute law and in the courts, another development of the theme of women's rights and empowerment.

Another motif in this novel is that of those law graduates—especially from the Ivy League schools—who do not enter public service but gravitate to corporate law, which offers them more money, power, potential political appointments, and prestige: "Harvard Law School," said Reed, "like the others in the same rank, preach service but make sure their graduates are not deluded by the sermons" (*IS*, 132). Reed talks about Richard Kahlenberg's *Broken Contract: A Memoir of Harvard Law School*,[17] in which the author discusses how the former president of Harvard, Derek Bok, "deplored the rush to corporate law," regretting that the brightest graduates did not use their talents for the good of the community (*IS*, 132). His worthwhile ideas and ideals were vitiated when he appointed a neoconservative as the new dean of the law school.

Throughout this novel selected quotations from John le Carré's novels coalesce to form a unified view of the meaning of spying. Essentially, spying, claims the writer, is self-destruction. Harriet Furst obsessively quotes le Carré and considers herself a spy against Schuyler Law School in her valiant attempt to gather evidence against a faculty that contributed to the condemnation of Betty Osborne, who turns out to be her daughter. In talking with Harriet, Kate deflects the discussion to sleuthing. "All we detectives do, amateur or professional, even private eyes, even the police, is change the direction of events" (*IS*, 218). Kate, too, has been an imperfect spy in ferreting out those who help and those who hinder the restoration of order from the chaos of crime, a perception acceptable to critics who analyze the universe of murder mystery and general investigation of other wrongs. In effect, both Kate and Reed have spent much of their individual and collective time in probing the motives and opportunities of those who—short of crime—create dissension by their social behavior and in attempting to help those who—like Betty—have been the hapless victims of injustice.

Some of the critics who indicted Reed for being "wimpish" in catering to Kate's whims and moods in many of the previous Fansler novels may find a refreshing change in the state of their marriage in *An Imperfect Spy*. Both Kate and Reed articulate that something is amiss in their heretofore idyllic wedded life, but at first neither can cite anything explicit. Early in the novel, Kate laments, "We used to understand each other. Now the best we can achieve is a rather alienated tolerance" (*IS*, 26).

Kate tells Reed that she is restless with being at an end but not yet at a beginning. She had had a dalliance with a colleague, but no consummation. At Schuyler Law School, she is attracted to Blair Whitson and wonders whether anything serious will develop in their relationship. Kate tells Reed that he is just as dear as always, but his electricity has vanished. Reed reacts by offering to resign from his law faculty if Kate wishes. It is curious that he makes no assertions about their marriage or any demands on Kate and is willing to make concessions without quid pro quo. It is Reed who reminds Kate that to anyone of intelligence and sensitivity, there are times when the old is without worth and the new is unimaginable. Kate eventually quips that they will grow old together, with their arteries hardening at the same pace. She later says that while sex is often a substitute for problems, friendship is indispensable, because friends can use conversation to rediscover their lives. In probing their attitudes, Reed tells Kate that teaching and becoming one of the smug, mostly "mediocre clump cemented together by the ease and superficial congeniality of our life" (*IS*, 186) was easier than working in the district attorney's office, where one had to be constantly on the alert. When Kate agrees that she felt the same as he did about academia, Reed protests that her environment is different. "You always had the challenge of being a woman, of being a feminist, of trying to change the system" (*IS*, 186).

At Schuyler, Reed is given an assistant, Bobby, a female student. Intuitively, Kate, discovering that Bobby is infatuated with Reed, tells

Bobby that the fixation will pass in time. At the novel's end, when Reed says tentatively, "I've got you back," Kate replies, "You've never lost me," and she says that she would have fought Bobby "like a tiger" for her man (*IS,* 204).

Carolyn Heilbrun wrote that Kate Fansler taught her that in a marriage "a relationship has a momentum, it must change and develop and will tend to move toward the point of greatest commitment" (*WWL,* 123). In *An Imperfect Spy,* the reader senses from the many conversations between Kate and Reed that their union will survive, grow, and move toward that apex of commitment.

At the end of this novel, Reed agrees with Harriet that without Kate and him, the Schuyler Law School would have preserved the status quo. "We just frightened them as a result of being there. We didn't infiltrate; we were just ourselves. Spies infiltrate" (*IS,* 226). The conclusion suggests that without infiltration, a spy is "imperfect," hence the title.

The Cross Novels: "Instrument[s] in Imaginative Expression"

The 11 mystery novels of Amanda Cross reveal the many phases and changes of the protagonist Kate Fansler, academic and sleuth. The younger Kate appears lonely, arch, and acerbic, even snobbish in often mentioning her affluent background. And she is insecure, especially with Frederick Clemance and other colleagues in *Poetic Justice* and in her imaginary friendship with Auden, refusing to meet him when she has the opportunity. Often, it seems, she resorts to alcohol and smoking for self-protection and isolation. Rather than "call in" favors, Kate invariably prefers to "pull strings," since pulling empowers her. Smarting from her lack of power in academia because she is a woman, she does not recognize the power that stems from her cleverness and intelligence in solving puzzles and mysteries. She does not know how to wield power and believes that exercising power is unladylike. Estranged from her brothers, Kate makes no attempt to discuss and cope with their serious family difficulties and in time takes the easier path of developing a sound relationship with her niece and nephews, who are younger and more tractable.

In solving a murder case, Kate uses imagination, intuition, and judgment as she views the circumstances surrounding it, her ideas informed by her education but with a departure from traditional theories concerning the roles imposed by society on women. From the perspective of psychologist Albert Ellis, who formulated the theory of "rational-emotive therapy" (a system to train people to discriminate among a range of alternatives and thereby surrender most of their self-created emotional difficulties), Kate maintains an irrational belief that hers is the right way, the only way, and is loath to countenance other standards, especially in matters of ethical belief.[18] Lord Byron declared that Newstead Abbey, his ancestral castle, was highly conducive to a good marriage ("She in one wing and I in another"), and Kate's marriage may have survived because she and Reed spend much time apart. Perhaps because of their closer proximity in *An Imperfect Spy,* with both working for Schuyler Law School, Kate and Reed find problems in their marriage.

Although Kate is often witty and clever, she reveals snobbishness in criticizing the language of her colleagues and often uses words only for their effect. In *Poetic Justice,* Kate says, "Snobbism transforms itself into intelligent discrimination when practiced by ordinarily rational people" (*PJ,* 122–23). In *Death in a Tenured Position,* Kate shows her need for control when, in talking to a student about an interview, she insists on privacy: "If you agree to let the person see the transcript and correct it, and have the tape back, I don't see why there should be a problem" (*DTP,* 119). Though couched in courteous language, Fansler actually seeks to limit the interviewer's range of freedom of expression and interpretation.

Yet, Kate Fansler is also portrayed as highly intelligent, with a phenomenal memory for literary allusions and the recital of passages from all of Virginia Woolf's novels. Kate is altruistic as she does her pro bono work in solving the crimes, puzzles, and mysteries at her own expense. Even her apartment is often available to the troubled, who are offered a drink, solace, and advice. She is deeply disturbed by academics who seize power to use it against colleagues and students and who tolerate mediocrity and compromise in their politicization of campus issues and education. In marrying, Kate reveals that a feminist can enjoy love and companionship with a man and still work for the equality of women.

As Kate grows older from 1964 to 1995, she mellows, often showing more empathy for those overwhelmed by their unhappy destiny, as shown in *Sweet Death, Kind Death* in the figure of Stevie Smith and in *The Players Come Again* in the portraits of Anne, Dorinda, and Nellie, wherein Kate transmits genuine feeling for women and their friendships.

As Carolyn Heilbrun herself says of Kate, "She is, oddly, no longer a fantasy figure but an aging woman who battles despair and, one hopes, with a degree of wit and humor, finds in the constant analysis of our ancient patriarchal ways, and in her sheer effrontery, a reason to endure" (*WWL,* 122).

As an ongoing series, the Kate Fansler novels show Amanda Cross, the alter ego of Carolyn Heilbrun, to be a quintessentially literary person who loves to quote, appreciates conversation, and delights in comedies of manners (*DD,* 187). Although not a P. D. James, who has been described as "the grand dame of fictional forensic pathology,"[19] Carolyn Heilbrun—with Amanda Cross—created a professor with a talent for urbane and sophisticated conversation. *Publisher's Weekly* reported in 1990 that "Cross remains queen of the American literary whodunit."[20] Despite her detractors, who do not appreciate her weak plots or the abundance of literary quotations and allusions, she is praised by many. Rebecca R. Butler writes, "In her dual role of professor and detective, Kate rings changes on the conventional detective puzzle. By drawing attention to the nature of the story and people's tendency to live by stories, Cross demonstrates that the detective formula can be transformed into an instrument of imaginative expression" (429).

Chapter Six

Recent Books:
More Scholarly Work, Biography

"Feminism, in the intellectual as well as the political sphere,
is at the very heart of a profound revolution"

This chapter addresses the nonfiction Carolyn Heilbrun published in 1981–95. It begins with *The Representation of Women in Fiction,* edited with Margaret R. Higonnet. Heilbrun explains in the introduction that feminist criticism in fiction was selected as a theme because in the novel and the novella the expression of true diversity is possible. Topics such as the artist as heroine, fictional consensus and female causalities, liberty and sorority and misogyny and people like Clara Middleton, George Sand, and Jane Austen are featured in some essays.

Another book discussed in this chapter, *Writing a Woman's Life,* is considered a classic by some. In it, Heilbrun laments the lack of narratives by women in certain periods of history, stating that such narratives play the important role of presenting models of the possible ways women can live. She insists that women reject definitions of themselves made by men. In this book Heilbrun also discusses English mystery writer Dorothy Sayers, herself as Amanda Cross, the relationships of two well-known literary couples, and friendship between women. Finally, the book confronts the question of women aging as a means of liberation, especially from what has been called "female impersonation." Male-designed narratives for women, she writes, have not succeeded; she concludes by urging women to write their own scripts.

Hamlet's Mother and Other Women, the third book presented in this chapter, leads with its title essay, "The Character of Hamlet's Mother," where Heilbrun takes issue with some of the criticism of Hamlet's mother, Gertrude. Other chapters center on exemplary women, as Heilbrun calls them; literature and women; feminism and the profession of literature; and detective fiction.

The final book considered here is *The Education of a Woman: The Life of Gloria Steinem,* a study of the woman who transcended poverty and male bias to become a world-famous feminist. This book and the others considered here demonstrate Heilbrun's intensifying interest in how women both live their lives and write about them.

The Representation of Women in Fiction

The Representation of Women in Fiction is a selection of papers from the annual meeting of the English Institute in 1981, edited by Carolyn G. Heilbrun and Margaret R. Higonnet, published in 1983.[1] In the brief introduction, Heilbrun relates that this was the institute's fortieth meeting and that the program was the first devoted to feminist criticism. Six essays are collected, three of which were part of the feminist program, one essay a part of another program, and two requested for the volume. It is notable that J. Hillis Miller is the only male writer. Heilbrun includes in her introduction remarks from "Perspective" by Cleanth Brooks, professor emeritus from Yale University and well-known critic, who died in 1994. Brooks recalled how in years gone by, when the English Institute was held at Columbia University, several faculty wives, some of them well educated and intelligent, were relegated to hostess duties, such as pouring tea. He also recalled an anecdote concerning a "brilliant" lecture by Lionel Trilling about the cultural situation as viewed by the contemporary American intellectual. Following Trilling's speech, a woman in the audience noted that when he used "we," he never spoke to "her condition" or to that of her friends, meaning that Trilling always excluded women from his reflections on intellectual matters. Unfortunately, Trilling's response is not included, but Heilbrun says that her erstwhile mentor, as always, was reported to have been both "gracious" and "polite."

In her introduction, Heilbrun praises Edward Said, critic of comparative literature and colleague at Columbia University, who for his 1978 volume of the English Institute commissioned an article from Catherine Stimpson, well-known feminist and theorist.

Heilbrun mentions that it was no surprise that this first program with its theme of feminist criticism was limited to fiction, since it is only in the novel and in fiction's shorter forms that "true diversity is possible," an idea of Mikhail Bakhtin, Russian literary theorist and philosopher of language, who said that the novel would continue to develop, that it would not desist from discussing what many might consider to be inappropriate themes. Bakhtin, however, never considered the discourse of feminism, says Heilbrun.

The articles collected in this book include one on the novel *Persuasion* by Jane Austen; one on George Sand and the novel of the female pastoral; one on the artist as heroine and the fiction of Katherine Mansfield; one on fictional consensus and female causalities; a provocative article by Jane Marcus titled "Liberty, Sorority, Misogyny," in which she discusses at length the work of Virginia Woolf; and a contribution by Miller on Clara Middleton, the heroine in George Meredith's novel *The Egoist.*

Discussion of these articles isn't pertinent to an examination of Heilbrun's work, but it can be said that all of them contain motifs that have absorbed Heilbrun for her entire professional life—women and feminism in literature.

Writing a Woman's Life

Published in 1988, Carolyn Heilbrun's *Writing a Woman's Life* turned out to be one of her best sellers. Its motifs are kaleidoscopic: women ignored in literature or depicted narrowly from a male viewpoint; literary figures of women who have rejected the traditional roles that society mandated for them; myths and realities of marriage; friendships and relationships among women; aging; power; Amanda Cross and Kate Fansler; and Heilbrun's life and other writings. Writing the lives of women is a corrective. Because men have largely failed to write about women's lives or have written about them from a male perspective, it is incumbent on women to write narratives about themselves and other women and to salute those women writers—like George Sand, Virginia Woolf, George Eliot, and Dorothy Sayers—who have already done so, who have lived unconventional lives of courage and independence. Women need to make their perceptions central as they write their own scripts.

Heilbrun strikes this chord in her medley of ideas: "The choices and pain of the women who did not make a man the center of their lives seemed unique, because there were no models of the lives they wanted to live, no exemplars, no stories. These choices, this pain, those stories, and how they may be more systematically faced, how, in short, one may find the courage to be an 'ambiguous woman' are what I want to examine in this book" (*WWL,* 31).

In focusing on women who have no text or narratives of their own, Heilbrun postulates a methodology for not only biography but criticism as well. As Betty Friedan writes in *The Fountain of Age* about this book, "Carolyn Heilbrun discusses the kind of shifts it took—and still takes—

for women to stop living as 'female impersonators' or 'heroines' of male romance, and discover instead 'new stories for women.'"[2]

In her discussion of narratives and women, Heilbrun cites four ways of writing a woman's life—in autobiography, biography, fiction, and the writing of a life in advance of living it (writing it, imagining it, and then following that course). Of course, it would seem that there are many more genres or approaches. Fiction, Heilbrun says, is excluded from her consideration in this book because it has already been probed by the literary critics of a new generation of feminists. She harks back to the 1970s when women's biographies and autobiographies were beginning to be published in quantum numbers. Yet even then some women writers found it difficult to express the rage, despair, and pain of their lives.

Heilbrun points to the dismay May Sarton felt over her *Plant Dreaming Plant* once she saw that none of the anger or despair she had felt in her life was expressed in the book. And Heilbrun looks at Eudora Welty's memoir, *One Writer's Beginnings,* finding Welty to be too much the perfect gentlewoman. The inability to express anger, Heilbrun asserts, results in the denial of control and power for women. When *Three Guineas* by Virginia Woolf was published, it was condemned expressly for its anger and its strident tone. Women have shunned power for many reasons, but Heilbrun cautions women to think of and pursue power. "However unhappy the concept of power and control may make idealistic women, they delude themselves if they believe that the world and the condition of the oppressed can be changed without acknowledging it" (*WWL,* 16). Heilbrun might have further added, "and using it as motivation for action." Without power, she continues, women deny themselves narratives, texts, and plots, among other avenues, all of which help them to assume power and, most important, exert control over their own lives. Heilbrun alludes to Deborah Cameron, an English linguistic theorist, who inveighs against males for defending their power and insisting that "'Sex differentiation must be rigidly upheld by whatever means are available, for men can be men only if women are unambiguously women.'"[3]

Women have been sentimentalized in many biographies, and they themselves in autobiographical narratives have found it impossible to admit achievement, the presence of ambition, or the fact that their accomplishment resulted from their own efforts, *vide* the lives of the indefatigable social worker Jane Addams, the famous muckraker Ida Tarbell, and writer Charlotte Perkins Gilman. Contrariwise, in private journals and letters, women use a completely different voice.

The last idea in the introduction of *Writing a Woman's Life* focuses on biography as genre, with Heilbrun quoting Roland Barthes on biography as "'a novel that dare not speak its name'" (*WWL,* 28). Biographies have been considered works of fiction since biography has been written by men or women who have their own perspective. This approach to biography as fiction is also the thrust of an article by Heilbrun entitled "Is Biography Fiction?" which appeared in the journal *Soundings* in 1993.[4] The well-known example used in this article had been included in *Writing a Woman's Life,* with Phyllis Rose the source.[5] The example is given of Quentin Bell's biography of his aunt Virginia Woolf, wherein he catalogues her illness and reliance on her husband Leonard Woolf and neglects her writings. In her article, Heilbrun writes, "Along came Phyllis Rose and writes a biography of Woolf as a feminist and a woman writer profoundly aware not only of the disabilities of her own sex, but also of the price society has paid, in wars, fascism, oppression, for the acting out of destructive, male-centered ideas supported by the system we call patriarchy" ("Biography," 299). Although many men like Quentin Bell and like Gordon Haight on George Eliot have written one-dimensional biographies of women, women, too, have sometimes done the same to men, for example, Catherine Drinker Bowen, author of the well-known *Yankee from Olympus: Justice Holmes and His Family.*

Since the concept of biography underwent profound changes in the two decades leading up to 1988, writes Heilbrun, biographers of women especially faced the new burden of choosing among several interpretations, reinventing the lives of their subjects and intuiting their choices and pain, areas that are not easily accessible and that need, therefore, to be carefully plumbed.

Women who did not seek their identity from men faced pain and difficult choices. They were atypical; no models or stories existed to help them define their lives. To explore the pain, the choices, the stories, and the courage to be ambiguous women is Heilbrun's major concern in this book. Heilbrun's first choice in presenting an "ambiguous" woman is George Sand, French novelist, who wore men's clothes and whose affair with Frederic Chopin, Polish pianist and composer, was immortalized by the scandal of their liaison in Mallorca, Spain. Sand—brilliant, courageous, energetic, charming, and passionate—lived life on her own terms. Heilbrun quotes the remarks of Henry James to Gustave Flaubert, famous French novelist, that "'the moral of George Sand's tale, the beauty of what she does for us, is not the extension she gives to the feminine nature, but the richness that she adds to the masculine'" (*WWL,*

36). Flaubert commented that one had to know George Sand well to see the degree of the feminine in "that great man." Stories, not lives, Heilbrun believes, serve as models. The story of George Sand is such an exemplum, although Heilbrun thinks that a biography of Sand from a suitably feminist perspective has yet to be written. T. S. Eliot, with all of his indecisions and confusions, is depicted by British biographer Peter Ackroyd as having the choice of several options that might be suitable to him; as a male, Eliot had a script to follow. The women of his time, however—Virginia Woolf, in particular—had no such luxury.

It is Heilbrun's belief, too, that women must share the stories of their lives, their aspirations, and their fantasies, even the unacceptable ones. She insists, "We must stop reinscribing male words and rewrite our ideas about what Nancy Miller calls a female impulse to power, as opposed to the erotic impulse which alone is supposed to impel women. We know we are without a text, and must discover one" (*WWL,* 44). When women exchange stories, when they read and talk together about their hopes, possibilities, and accomplishments, female narratives are discovered. If women do not meet and discuss their lives openly, they will not develop their own narratives. Only when women surrender their isolation and bondage to the narratives of men will there be the possibility of narratives in the lives of women.

Spending an entire chapter on Dorothy Sayers, including her life and a commentary on her female sleuth Harriet Vane and her friend and eventual husband, Lord Peter Wimsey, Heilbrun merges her interest in feminism and women with her enjoyment in reading and writing detective stories. Sayers, somewhat like Heilbrun, was a scholar, a fiercely self-reliant woman who refused to fit into the matrix that society imposed— and a writer of detective novels. In many of her interviews and many times in her writing, Heilbrun pays homage to the influence of Sayers. "It is impossible to overestimate the importance of her novels in my own life," she says (*WWL,* 51).

In alluding to the 1981 biography of Sayers by the Englishman James Brabazon, Heilbrun suggests that his view of his famous subject is myopic. In Sayers's writings, Heilbrun perceives wit, intelligence, a female community, and especially a moral universe, all suggesting a "possible" life, a model for other women. In the detective novels, Sayers created a fantasy, but not a romantic fantasy, which society programmed for women. Brabazon fails to note the existence of such a realm, writes Heilbrun, and depicts Sayers as passively accepting her fate and stating that she might have been happier had she been pretty, married, and

borne lots of children—all of these ideas suggesting Brabazon's stereotypical mindset about women. Heilbrun's comment on his interpretation
of Sayers is ironically astute: "He notes that Sayers lacked the necessary
accoutrements for the successful enactment of a male-designed script"
(*WWL*, 52).

It was Erik Erikson, the American psychoanalyst, who used the term
moratorium to suggest that in the lives of gifted people there is a period of
fallowness or indecision, say before age 30, when nothing seems to be
happening, no goals defined or reached, but that actually these talented
artists are preparing for the time of activity. Heilbrun indicts Brabazon
for not recognizing the "moratorium" in the life of Sayers and for misap-
prehending her when he wrote that because Sayers was not attractive to
men, she had to fall back on her intellect, as though sexuality and intelligence were mutually exclusive.

In having a child out of wedlock, Sayers, writes Heilbrun, asserted
independence of spirit at a time when social mores condemned women
for such an act. Sayers refused, as well, to dress to satisfy others, and for
these reasons she was considered a maverick.

Heilbrun perceives that Sayers had to first create the very charming,
accommodating, and humorous Lord Peter Wimsey before she could
design Harriet Vane. In *Gaudy Night,* one of the best known of Sayers's
mysteries, Peter and Harriet decide to marry. Heilbrun believes that with
Gaudy Night, "Sayers produced the novel she had prepared all of her life
to write. She had completed her task of transforming the detective story
and embodying her vision of intellectual integrity in a woman character"
(*WWL*, 55). Harriet Vane is known and enjoyed by many readers who
recognize her intellectual acuity, her autonomy, and her "unwomanli-
ness." In overcoming a "bruised" heart, Harriet does not rely on a
"manly" bosom but rather on physical activity, work, and an instant
"acquisition of wealth." Like many readers and critics, Heilbrun believes
that Harriet Vane's many contours are also those of Sayers.

Although there is much in this chapter on Sayers that readers may
agree with, Heilbrun seems to follow Brabazon's conclusions in one
respect—she avers that Sayers refused the honor of accepting a Lambeth
Degree, bestowed by the Archbishop of Canterbury, because she was
aware of the sinfulness of her son's birth and was afraid that this fact
might be uncovered. What some readers find distasteful is Heilbrun's
comment that "We, who now know all the facts, may well decide that it
was in her sinfulness, rather than in her devoutness, that her true destiny
as a woman is revealed" (*WWL*, 59). Heilbrun presents no facts to sup-

port this assertion, and the sentence is filled with ambiguity. Yet Heilbrun's conclusion is sound when she says that Sayers's life "teaches us about the possible hidden lives of accomplished women who were educated enough to have had a choice and brave enough to have made one" (*WWL*, 59).

Heilbrun next shifts to those women, mainly poets, who lifted the constraints against women's writing in their poetry, essays, books, and interviews, mainly by finding a way to express their anger. Although some of the poetry of Anne Sexton, Maxine Kumin, and Adrienne Rich, among others, has been criticized for its confessionalism, these poets wrote about their own lives, about personal rebellion and the recognition of a too-ready acceptance of female servitude. With their poetry of enslavement in marriage and motherhood and their interest in lesbianism and ethnicity, such women writers sounded a call to arms for others, defying the strictures of T. S. Eliot against use of the personal.

In this chapter, Heilbrun defines "her" generation—for whom World War II became a metaphoric prism—and concludes by citing Audre Lorde, who was of the post–World War II generation, a self-styled "'black lesbian feminist warrior poet'" (*WWL*, 74). At the end of her life (she died in 1992), Lorde, in Heilbrun's words, "writing of illness, woman as victim and survivor, and the sole saving grace of female friendship, speaks, across race, national, or class boundaries for what is now *her* generation of women" (*WWL*, 75). Lorde, indeed, broke many molds. Heilbrun reminds readers that black women writers of this generation have bestowed on women their first compelling texts on female friendship—Toni Morrison's *Sula* (1973), for example, and Lorde's *Cancer Journals* (1980).

Marriage is a major theme in chapter 4, where Heilbrun calls wedlock "the most persistent of myths imprisoning women, and misleading those who write of women's lives" (*WWL*, 77). No longer does a woman's status depend on the man she marries. Marriage patterns since the mid-1950s have changed, often as the result of women's independence economically and socially and their freedom from the assumptions of motherhood.

Heilbrun discusses the crucial component of a revolutionary marriage, one in which work is the center of the couple's lives in an environment that supports each alone and both together. Often, women, like those in a Jane Austen novel, seek a marriage of upward mobility. Virginia Woolf's marriage to Leonard was the reverse, but these two people were sui generis. Heilbrun contends that in a successful marriage there is equality in work and money. In many cases, the men are nurturers. In light of the many divorces in the contemporary United States, Heilbrun wonders whether marriage can be redefined or whether legalized unions are becoming passé, but she does not elaborate. She believes that servitude is suggested in a woman's exchanging her maiden name for her husband's, yet Carolyn Gold herself adopted the name of James Heilbrun.

Marriage in fiction, when it has been discussed, has generally been presented in its romantic guise, says Heilbrun, for if it were not, women would not be attracted to the state and its usefulness to the patriarchy would be ended. Love, which Heilbrun states is a "temporary togetherness," fails to prepare women for the constrictions to come after the marriage ceremony. Today, though, women need not marry their lovers and need not consider, as in the past, their sole destiny to be marriage. Unlike Anna Karenina, who suffered isolation when in love with Count Vronsky, women today in a liaison need not fear ostracism. In the first half of the nineteenth century, women were, of course, considered chattel when they married, surrendering every personal and economic right and becoming subservient to their husbands. No longer is marriage legal servitude in the Western world, yet women in marriage need new definitions about the actualities of the wedded state; there is need, says Heilbrun, for narration, and no one has yet written a new marriage plot.

Again, Heilbrun discusses the marriage of Virginia and Leonard Woolf, in which Leonard failed to understand his wife, as recent scholarship has revealed. Ultimately, though, Heilbrun agrees that "marrying Leonard was the wisest thing Virginia did. I believe that he made her writing life possible" (*WWL*, 90). In her liaison with George Henry Lewes, George Eliot had that which Auden explains marriage should be: a mutual respect between equals. Yet Eliot was not able to create a strong and satisfying marriage in her fiction. Passion does not endure; Heilbrun cites its obvious absence in the marriage of Virginia Woolf, who never revealed details of her life with Leonard, yet once admitted a significant detail about the endurance of this marriage—that when Leonard entered a room, she never knew what he would say. This element of surprise in marriage is one that Amanda Cross often alludes to in the strong marriage of Kate Fansler and Reed Amhearst.

Learning the language to understand and describe successful marriage is crucial, especially in writing the narratives of achieving women, Heilbrun believes. In speaking of reinventing marriage, she means a rebirth in middle age of wedlock. She offers Stanley Cavell's book

Pursuits of Happiness[6] as possibly the best manual of marriage ever printed. Heilbrun cites one of Cavell's axioms about marriage: "'in God's intention a meet and happy conversation is the chiefest and noblest end of marriage'" (*WWL*, 94).

The final point Heilbrun makes about marriage here is that biographers often view it from the exterior only, through the romantic lens designed by the patriarchy. In middle age, a remarriage is the revitalization of this rite, one that will encompass friendship, conversation, and the equality of quests for both men and women. In such a successful union, no debate or challenge is excluded, and law and policy are unendurable concepts. Heilbrun's coda is the wise statement, "The rules, if any, are known only to the two players, who seek no public trophy" (*WWL*, 95).

Love and marriage between men and women have aspects that intertwine in many ways with friendship. Heilbrun devotes 12 pages to this close relationship between women, beginning with her remarks on the well-known friendship in the Bible between two men: David and Jonathan. When Jonathan is killed in a battle led by David, David laments his friend's death. "Thy love to me was wonderful, passing the love of women." Heilbrun cites an excerpt from an essay on friendship by the French writer Montaigne, who felt that "'the ordinary capacity of women is inadequate for that communion and fellowship which is the nurse of this sacred bond'" (*WWL*, 101). Montaigne goes on to stipulate that could women be capable of deep friendships with men, the fusion of body would engage the entire man, resulting in a fuller, more complete friendship. It is Heilbrun's contention that men form bonds or friendships in the "realms of power," contradistinctive to women, who forge "societies of consolation." Intimacy is femaleness. Women have traditionally been relegated to nurture men, to feed and comfort them, like servants, and to be available for the marital duty of sex. "Men have guessed, therefore, that true friendship, in some way resembles ideal marriage, though neither friendship nor marriage has attained the ideal: friendship has too much resembled for men the camaraderie of battle, for women the consolations of passivity; marriage has owed too much to romance, too little to friendship" (*WWL*, 102).

For Heilbrun, coming closest to any ideal of friendship, since she talks about this example at length, is that of Vera Brittain and Winifred Holtby, contemporaries of Dorothy Sayers at Oxford, whose friendship persisted from 1920 to 1937, until Holtby's death. Brittain married, but Holtby did not, yet this change in Brittain's status did not impair the strength of their friendship, as it does for many women who marry. Brittain wrote of their profound friendship in *Testament of Youth* and later in *Testament of Friendship*. Holtby became a successful novelist. While Brittain did manage some writing, the demands of a conventional marriage with children deprived her of much of the time and energy she might have put into it. Theirs was no lesbian relationship, although the two were accused of this, with Winifred's sardonic response being, "Too, *too* Chelsea!" (referring to the overly sophisticated people in that part of London who would not be disturbed by the idea of such a relationship). Vera and Winifred felt work to be important, spent much time in writing when they were together, and always accorded each other freedom and understanding. Winifred wrote, "'Without work I am nothing'" (*WWL*, 103).

Both Brittain and Holtby were also enriched by a host of friends, not isolated by or consumed with their own friendship. This deep-rooted involvement is a veritable matrix for friendship between women. Heilbrun lauds Holtby's *Women and a Changing Civilization,* which she finds "almost unbearably contemporary" (*WWL*, 106). Heilbrun supports her belief by quoting a paragraph of Holtby's book, which shows that her questioning of gender limits and definitions together with her rejection of stereotypes and generalizations concerning men and women are surprisingly modern. In this book, Holtby offers the caveat that men and women not reduce themselves to dull patterns but instead permit each other release to their infinite variety. She claims there is no litmus test for either masculine or feminine characteristics or for "normal" sexual relationships but only "vast generalizations," all of which generate "indescribable" suffering" (*WWL*, 106).[7]

Heilbrun concludes this chapter with a reference to Adrienne Rich, who believes that "Eroticism, or energy, continues between any friends who share a passion for their work and a body of political ideas" (*WWL*, 108). Biographies of women must search for friends who participate in such a vision.

In limiting some of the virtues she attributes to women in their friendships, such as "softness" and "gentle affection," Heilbrun excludes men, who, she says, delegate these qualities to women. Gay men, particularly, take exception to her interpretations and exclusions. There is a body of books and films that show many men in their homosexual friendships revealing these very same virtues—*Maurice* by E. M. Forster and the short stories of David Leavitt, among others.

The content of the penultimate chapter in *Writing a Woman's Life,* a personal narrative that Carolyn Heilbrun writes to explain and justify her use of the nom de plume Amanda Cross, has already been discussed in this volume in the chapters on Heilbrun's life and on the Amanda Cross novels. Perhaps the only additional point worthy of mention is the epigraph to chapter 6, a quote from Gloria Steinem: "'[Marilyn Monroe] was a female impersonator; we are all trained to be female impersonators'" (*WWL*, 109). The "blonde bombshell," as Marilyn Monroe was called, was in fact a double impersonator. Like most women of her generation, she grew into a role imposed by the American patriarchal society as it created its own Galateas. Monroe was shaped again into the Hollywood-conceived role of sexual goddess, who would, during her lifetime and beyond, become an icon for many Americans. Steinem is saying that the male power structure has attempted to clone "us" into a figment of "their" vision, a flawed and skewered femininity.

The last chapter of *Writing a Woman's Life* is a quietly impassioned modus vivendi for the aging woman, freed at last from all constraints that society and woman herself have imposed. At 50, Virginia Woolf began writing *The Years* and *Three Guineas,* which even today, writes Heilbrun, offend and even insult some male critics. Having reached this age, Woolf at last had the courage to express the mounting anger of many years against the patriarchy. "It is perhaps only in old age," Heilbrun believes, "certainly past fifty, that women can stop being female impersonators, can grasp the opportunity to reverse their most cherished principles of 'femininity'" (*WWL,* 126).

Heilbrun contends that few aged women think that the advancing years confer power on them, as Isak Dinesen, the Danish writer, believed—that once women are old and finished with the "business of being women," strength can be released and changed into mighty power. Too long have women lived with the idea of "closure." "When the hope for closure is abandoned," Heilbrun insists, "when there is an end to fantasy, adventure for women will begin" (*WWL*, 130).

Biographers, writes Heilbrun at the very end of this book, despite the lack of available and acceptable narratives for women, must persist in searching through the disguises of aging and aged women to find ultimately the woman herself.

In *Writing a Woman's Life,* after presenting her thesis that male-designed narratives for women have not succeeded in restraining highly talented, courageous women from living their own iconoclastic lives, Heilbrun urges women to write their own texts, scripts, narratives. Although at times Heilbrun scatters her birdshot over too much terrain, overall she succeeds in forging a strong argument for the cause of women living their own lives without conforming to a "romantic" identity designed by a powerful patriarchy.

Arie De Knecht found this book flawed in its condemnation of all males. "Heilbrun," he says, "attacks the patriarchy too sweepingly. Her simplistic methodology ignores the men who over the years have advanced the cause of feminism. Such an omission weakens and even trivializes her argument and alienates the good fellows who have worked in the trenches and call themselves feminists. Heilbrun also ignores people like Antonia Fraser, who is a well-known English biographer, among others."[8]

Another viewpoint is expressed by Wendy Martin, chairwoman of the English Department, Claremont Graduate School, who writes in the *New York Times Book Review,* "If Carolyn Heilbrun's astute and provocative book had been available twenty-five years ago, most of my friends and I could have been spared considerable grief. But it required the women's movement and the feminist scholarship of the last two decades to provide the political and intellectual scaffolding for this collection of wise and witty essays. . . . *Writing a Woman's Life* is accessible, engaging and compelling. It will be read with great pleasure and interest by specialists and general readers alike and should be required reading for all women before they turn twenty-one."[9]

Hamlet's Mother and Other Women

Carolyn Heilbrun's *Hamlet's Mother and Other Women,* which appeared in 1990, is a pastiche of 21 essays that, with one exception (the title article, published in 1957), were written between 1972 and 1988. It consists of an introduction and five sections—"The Character of Hamlet's Mother," "Exemplary Women," "Literature and Women," "Feminism and the Profession of Literature," and "Detective Fiction"—on which I will offer commentary, focusing on an article or two from each section.

Introduction   In the introduction to *Hamlet's Mother and Other Women,* Heilbrun defines her understanding of the term *feminism* in a sort of response to younger women who deride feminism even though their careers might not have been possible without it. "A feminist," writes Heilbrun, "as I use the word, questions the gender arrangements in society and culture (all societies and cultures) and works to change them; the desired transformation gives more power to women while simultaneously challenging both forms and the legitimacy of power as it is now established."[10]

"The Character of Hamlet's Mother"   In the flagship article, "The Character of Hamlet's Mother," first published in the *Shakespeare Quarterly,* Heilbrun states that the character of Gertrude, Hamlet's mother, has received insufficient critical attention. To bolster her argument, Heilbrun quotes passages from three Shakespearean critics, all men. A. C. Bradley, Harley Granville-Barker, and Dover Wilson, respectively, dismiss Gertrude as a sloth; a narcissist, fading and withering; and a shallow, tepid optimist. These three critics fail to perceive Gertrude's lust, an important part of her character. It is a tragic flaw that leads to her incestuous marriage to Claudius, which shocks Hamlet and dashes his hopes for the throne; without Gertrude's lust, there would be no play. The three critics characterize Gertrude as vacillating and weak rather than intelligent, determined, sexually passionate, and strong. Heilbrun argues to the contrary, calling attention to Gertrude's succinct speech and her loving manner to Hamlet, whom she urges to remain in Denmark, where he is loved.

Heilbrun evidences the queen's precision of speech in a scene with Polonius when Gertrude says, "More matter with less art" (II.ii.95), and again later during the play with, "The lady doth protest too much, methinks" (III.ii.240). Her greeting to Rosencrantz and Guildenstern and her words to Ophelia reveal the queen to be gracious and kind, certainly not passive and inane. Heilbrun sees in this speech of Gertrude not only her recognition of lust as a sin but also her admission of this offense:

> O Hamlet, speak no more!
> Thou turn'st mine eyes into my very soul,
> And there I see such black and grained spots
> As will not leave their tinct. (III.iv.88–91)

In her interpretation of Gertrude, Heilbrun also rejects the assumption by certain critics "who have accepted the Ghost's word 'adulterate' in the modern meaning" (*HM,* 17), concluding that Gertrude and Claudius were lovers before the elder Hamlet's death. She reminds readers that in Shakespeare's day (the Elizabethan day) adultery referred to any objectionable sexual relationship, certainly an incestuous one. The Ghost believed the marriage to be unchaste, but the Elizabethan audience would not categorically assume that there was an unchaste affair between these two when the elder Hamlet was alive.

Heilbrun in this essay presents her reading of Gertrude's character beyond that of some male critics by depicting the queen as a key figure

in Shakespeare's drama, not vapid but strong and intelligent, sensitive to
the feelings of Ophelia and Hamlet, and recognizing herself to be a slave
to passion, which has effectively barred young Hamlet from becoming
king. Clearly, Heilbrun reads the character of Gertrude from a feminist
point of view.

"Exemplary Women"   In this second part of the book Heilbrun discusses Margaret Mead, the well-known anthropologist; Freud's daughters (both real—Anna Freud—and figurative—a group of women psy-
choanalysts); writers and mutual friends Vera Brittain and Winifred
Holtby; and Virginia Woolf. While Heilbrun's discussion of each of the
above subjects is informative, only Virginia Woolf, one of her favorites,
will be discussed here.

In her long career in teaching and in writing, Heilbrun has been con-
sumed with Virginia Woolf's life and literature. Her 1982 essay "Virginia
Woolf and James Joyce: Ariadne and the Labyrinth" refers to Diane
Fortuna's 1972 article "The Labyrinth as Controlling Image in Joyce's *A
Portrait of the Artist as a Young Man.*"[11] Fortuna cites Joyce's awareness of
Arthur Evans's discovery of the royal palace of Minos at Knossos, Crete,
and of the labyrinth. Heilbrun also cites the role of Jane Harrison, a
Greek scholar at Oxford, who knew of the excavations and who, as a
friend of Woolf, impressed the novelist with the Ariadne-Theseus-
Minotaur myth.

In the midst of writing *Mrs. Dalloway,* Woolf began reading, sporadi-
cally, James Joyce's *Ulysses,* about which Woolf records in her diary, "'An
illiterate, underbred book, it seems to me: the book of a self-taught
working man & we all know how distressing they are, how egotistic,
insistent, raw, striking and ultimately nauseating'" (*HM,* 69). Woolf
often speaks and writes in revelation of her snobbishness. Heilbrun
notes, "How could [Woolf] have failed to perceive *Ulysses,* with its arrant
masculinity and seaminess, with its drinking and swearing and eating
and fornicating, but as a direct attack on her own aims for *Mrs.
Dalloway?*" (*HM,* 71). Of course, Heilbrun dismisses the claims of
William York Tindall that *Mrs. Dalloway* was an imitation of *Ulysses* or
that Woolf was somehow indebted to Joyce.

Heilbrun quotes several variants of the myth of the labyrinth from
Fortuna and the *Oxford Classical Dictionary* in her analysis of the use of
this myth by, and its influence on, Joyce and Woolf. Joyce is concerned
with Daedalus while Woolf is aware of Ariadne, who aided Theseus in

his return after he had killed the Minotaur, and of his eventual abandonment of her.

Joyce, Heilbrun makes clear, re-created the "old cosmology," while Woolf endeavored to "invent, or reinvent," a new one. She further insists that Joyce, though modern in his technique, was "profoundly conservative" in his art. Joyce's characters are not conscious of the "ancient texts" they discarded, but Woolf's characters are. Woolf's world exists beyond the labyrinth; like Ariadne, she could create her own life beyond the maze. Heilbrun declares, "Nowhere do Joyce and Woolf divide so sharply as in their portrayal of women and the destinies of women" (*HM*, 81). Joyce follows the male version of the Pasiphae (wife of Minos) story, while Woolf follows Ariadne's destiny. Joyce's theme is the search for the father; Woolf follows the search for the mother. "Woolf set out to create a new and female text," asserts Heilbrun (*HM*, 81).

Trilling's commentary on a number of Joyce's letters is also offered by Heilbrun to show Joyce to be distant and narcissistic, especially about his art, and to contrast the Irish genius with the English novelist, who was more open in her diary and letters. Heilbrun also quotes Phillippe Sollers, author of the 1977 essay "Joyce & Co.,"[12] in which he states that women provided Joyce all of his life with money so that he could write (*HM*, 89).

Heilbrun concludes her essay on these two famous writers with these words: "Woolf went in search of Ariadne, and Joyce threaded again the old labyrinth" (*HM*, 86). Clearly, throughout the essay Heilbrun tilts toward Woolf, whom she has always considered a feminist, and away from Joyce, whom she considers quite the opposite—as having a patriarchal view of women in a quintessential form.

Readers may find the article provocative; certainly, it seems well researched, but Helen Vendler of Harvard University takes exception to many of its features, especially what she refers to as Heilbrun's "bizarre remarks" that if Leonard Woolf had taken Virginia to a Freudian psychiatrist, her novels would not have been written. Vendler also objects to Heilbrun's statements that while Woolf lacked confidence, male writers did not. "Has she read Keats's letters to his preface to 'Endymion?' Wallace Stevens's journals? Hopkins's retreat notes? Herbert's poems?"[13] Vendler also takes Heilbrun to task for using Sollers's statement concerning women's subsidy of Joyce, declaring that Heilbrun says nothing about Leonard Woolf's economic support of Virginia. Finally, Vendler scoffs at Heilbrun's allusions to Woolf's "raiding the inarticulate" because she discovered new ideas while Joyce wanted only to find a new way to express the "same things." "If this," stresses Vendler, "is what a conversion to feminism does to the truth of Joyce's subversive anti-imperial reimagining of the English novel, then such conversions are for literary criticism, lamentable" (Vendler, 23).

"Literature and Women"   This part of the book consists of articles on Penelope, wife of Ulysses; marriage in English literature (from 1873 to 1944); Virginia Woolf's *To the Lighthouse;* Louisa May Alcott's *Little Women;* and May Sarton. I'll discuss here "What Was Penelope Unweaving?"

In this essay, first published in 1985, Heilbrun surveys women who have weaved in stories and in myths—Penelope, wife of Odysseus, who wove and unwove a shroud for her father-in-law; Philomena, sister-in-law of Tereus, who ravished her and cut out her tongue to prevent her from incriminating him, but whose guilt was woven into Philomena's tapestry, to be read by her sister, Procne; and Ariadne, who gave Theseus a thread to lead him out of the Cretan labyrinth. Weaving, writes Heilbrun, was speech for women, their language, their story, and their response to the silence mandated by the patriarchy.

Heilbrun places Penelope at center stage as she waits for the return of Odysseus from the Trojan War. Ironically, the shroud Penelope is weaving acts as symbol for release and freedom from marrying one of the many suitors who believed Odysseus dead. Of course, Penelope unraveled at night that which she wove during the day. Heilbrun quotes several translations of the *Odyssey* to remind the reader of germane details. Telemachus, Penelope's son, is as officious as the suitors when he dismisses his mother twice, once saying, "'For mine is the power in the household'" (*HM,* 123). She is doubly punished, by her own son as well as by the suitors.

In the weaving and unweaving of the shroud, Penelope creates for herself freedom of choice. She had to invent her scheme, writes Heilbrun, because she had no text or narrative as a guide. "In literature and out," says Heilbrun, "through all recorded history, women have lived by a script that they did not write" (*HM,* 126). Now Penelope is composing a text. As Heilbrun has expressed elsewhere a number of times, women were in thrall to an erotic plot, a courtship plot, and a marriage plot; when married, they found their story finished. The patriarchy's chief source of power, she contends, has been anchored in "unquestioned narratives."

Heilbrun's basic, bedrock belief is that our lives are lived through the texts that have formed us and that we must build on them to make new fictions and so new lives. She implicitly laments that the traditional female plot brings security and social acceptance and, for the young, the ego satisfaction of being the object of male yearning.

Like Penelope, writes Heilbrun, many women no longer weave the same pattern or follow an old text but begin a new tapestry on the old. Penelope's story thus becomes a new narrative in the unweaving, suggesting choice, though accompanied by fear and anxiety over the unknown. When Odysseus returns, he listens first to Penelope, who, despite staying in Ithaca, relates a tale of new experiences, and this new text is the point at which her unweaving stops and her new narrative begins.

In this article, Heilbrun breathes life into Penelope, who is often simply dismissed as a victim of the importunate suitors, a faithful and patient soul, while actually she is resourceful and crafty (like Odysseus), refusing to submit to her fate (the old script). Here, with Heilbrun's reinterpretation, Penelope is reborn, refashioned, and rejuvenated.

"Feminism and the Profession of Literature"   In this section Heilbrun includes essays on literature, women and men in literature, and feminist criticism in departments of literature as well as her address as president of the Modern Language Association in 1984 on the politics of mind concerning women in the university. From this array of her articles, "Women, Men, Theories, and Literature," first published in 1981, is discussed.

"Women, Men, Theories, and Literature" remarks on the struggle that some professors of literature face when they insist that the only literature worth teaching is "quality" literature ("classics") as opposed to "popular" literature (trendy contemporary fiction). Popular literature is beneath the dignity of such teachers. Of course, as Amanda Cross, Heilbrun herself writes popular novels that are scoffed at by some traditionalists. Heilbrun quotes J. Hillis Miller, who believes in the "established canon" of literature, both English and American, and "'in the validity of the concepts of privileged texts. . . . I think it is more important to read Spenser, Shakespeare, or Milton than to read Borges in translation, or even, to say the truth, to read Virginia Woolf" (*HM*, 217). Of course, the reader, knowing Heilbrun's predilection for Virginia Woolf, can see that to her this remark is heresy.

Heilbrun discusses strategies to enliven the teaching and the study of literature; in so doing, she approves of Stanley Fish's idea of challenging the assumptions of "ordinary practices." One mode of such challenge, writes Heilbrun, is the use of feminist criticism, an approach on which she elaborates by presenting a number of examples from writers and critics who in effect use feminist criticism when they select and perceive a literary work from at least a second point of view.

When Heilbrun quotes from an article by Geoffrey Hartman concerning the attacks of critics against theories such as deconstruction, structuralism, revisionism, and Marxist and psychoanalytic criticism, which Hartman admits are viable approaches to literature, she notes that "feminism" is noticeably absent. "Language has been a powerful social force, male, that undermines the autonomy of the individual, female," writes Heilbrun (*HM, 222*). Hartman feels awkward with "aspects of feminist criticism" that lead to, in his words, "gendrification of literature." Heilbrun then cites English male novelists who do not feel uncomfortable in writing imagined fictions of women (W. M. Thackeray, Henry James, Thomas Hardy, E. M. Forster, and D. H. Lawrence, among others), in finding women's destiny a keener challenge than male adventuring.

Heilbrun recounts her experience of team teaching with Nancy Miller, who was trained by Michael Riffaterre at Columbia University's Department of French and Romance Philology in linguistic criticism, whereas Heilbrun was taught by Lionel Trilling to approach literature from the view of moral realism. Heilbrun transmits their excitement in sharing their different approaches and skills in interpreting literature through feminist criticism. Her idea for engendering excitement in the teaching of literature is a revolutionary new paradigm. "I am suggesting that feminism, in the intellectual as well as the political sphere, is at the very heart of a profound revolution" (*HM, 224*). In this way, the masterpieces of literature will become "newly vital." Professors who bridle at the use of "popular" in the classroom need to become aware of different approaches to the teaching of literature.

All in all, Heilbrun persuasively presents her case for the need for feminist criticism, almost likening this new approach, as she says, to Darwin's revolutionary theory of evolution. Helen Vendler, in reviewing eight books on women, one of them *Hamlet's Mother,* attacks this essay. She objects to Heilbrun's assertion that there is a distinction between the language of men and that of women: it is just not true. "Language is certainly a powerful force in the hands of anyone who uses it well, whether Jane Austen or Shakespeare, but it is of itself neither male nor female" (Vendler, 23). Responding to Heilbrun's views on the revolutionary approach to teaching, Vendler writes, "The description of 'feminist teaching,' as Heilbrun gives it, is just another version of the teaching of literature as propaganda—a method used earlier by other ideologues, on the right and left, for religious or political ends" (Vendler, 23).

"Detective Fiction" In this last part of *Hamlet's Mother* Carolyn Heilbrun discusses detective fiction. First she discusses a type of detective fiction, "The Detective Novel of Manners," for which she uses the acronym "DNOM." She defines the genre, which originated in England, where class, race, and manners are of quintessential importance. Class structure is the sine qua non of the DNOM; it concerns the white upper and middle classes and their accompanying moral and social principles. In a society where modes of behavior are fixed, murder or any other type of crime is censurable because it epitomizes a betrayal, an abandonment of society's trust.

Since the dissolution of the British colonial empire, the incoming waves of immigration, and the crumbling of the elitist structure in England, writing the DNOM is no longer possible. Dorothy Sayers is the best representative of the DNOM, says Heilbrun, and her *Gaudy Night* is her "most feminist novel." Choice, says Heilbrun, is the essential point of this novel, in which a number of Oxford women form a community for work. P. D. James believes that Sayers, like all first-class writers, created a recognizable world into which readers can escape for comfort. Heilbrun quotes Nina Auerbach, American critic, on *Gaudy Night* as a unique academic novel revealing the pleasure of the rigors of methodology and the clear seriousness of life at Oxford. Lord Peter Wimsey, unquestionably a feminist, solves the crime, an indication of some measure of women's insecurity at that time. Today, believes Heilbrun, Harriet Vane would herself solve the crime. Women readers are often drawn to Peter Wimsey by his feminism.

In citing the hard-boiled, anti-female American detective novel, Heilbrun concludes, "If those who eschew this genre of violence still write detective novels of moral people able to conceive of a moral universe, fighting for what seems right even when the system offers no rewards for such courage, they may be in the process of creating a new genre" (*HM,* 289).

"Gender and Detective Fiction" is a short essay in which Heilbrun defines males, females, and androgynes. Having a healthy sense of one's gender, contends Heilbrun, means being at ease with the body reflected in a mirror. As in other essays, Heilbrun compliments the British for having produced novels and especially mysteries that are more accepting of androgyny than those by Americans. If men acquire some so-called "feminine" characteristics, no one looks askance at them, but if the women adopt "masculine" characteristics, they are acrimoniously attacked. Yet there is hope, Heilbrun writes: "I think that this openness about the prison of gender is one of the detective novel's great claims to fame" (*HM*, 299).

Last, in the article "Sayers, Lord Peter, and Harriet Vane at Oxford," Heilbrun alludes to James Brabazon's biography of Dorothy Sayers, especially to his comment that she was "'a steam-roller in arguments.'" Heilbrun then presents excerpts of several Sayers letters from the rare books collection at Smith College library. These letters reflect a woman who disliked trivia, enjoyed discussions on serious subjects, loved Oxford, and found amusement in being the only woman taking an examination there. What is particularly interesting is Heilbrun's use of a quotation from Sayers's introduction to her translation of Dante's *Inferno,* a quote that Heilbrun believes has a bearing on the "moral center" of *Gaudy Night*—that we are not slaves to chance or environment, that good and evil are not just relative terms, that actions do matter, that with free will, choices can be made. These views have pleased many feminists.

Heilbrun considers it important to note that Lord Peter changes in *Gaudy Night,* as does Harriet Vane; it is a rare occurrence when two people can change together. Their marriage will be joyful. Heilbrun concludes with her observation that Sayers invented an extraordinary life and that "Harriet Vane is close to a unique creation in a literature where women writers before 1970 have rarely, if ever, given us women characters as independent as themselves" (*HM*, 310).

Hamlet's Mother puts forth a parade of various women, courageous in their unremitting struggle to create their own texts in a world of male hegemony. Such women collectively provide a model for those still unaware of the delights that will evolve from the struggle to awaken their own needs and sensibilities. If there is a keener awareness of men and women in some classrooms of America to accommodate teaching to the needs of both genders, Heilbrun has been a noteworthy catalyst through many of the ideas in this book.

The Education of a Woman: The Life of Gloria Steinem

The same year (1995) that Heilbrun published her eleventh detective novel, *An Imperfect Spy, The Education of a Woman: The Life of Gloria*

Steinem also appeared. With the publication of this book Heilbrun in a sense brought her career full circle as her longtime interests in biography and feminism conjoined. In this book on Steinem, Heilbrun writes, "I, as a biographer of a feminist, begin from the desire to write the life of a woman who became, simultaneously, the epitome of female beauty and the quintessence of female revolution."[14] She might have added that she selected a woman who wrote her own narrative. Some critics, nevertheless, might be surprised that instead of writing another book about women, feminism, and literature (the hallmark of her publications), Heilbrun agreed to write this authorized biography of a woman not essentially identified with literature. Heilbrun's intention was to examine how Steinem became Steinem, how she was transformed from the "intellectual pinup" woman of the 1970s into a spokeswoman for America's feminist movement.

Much of this latest book by Heilbrun seems a pastiche of Steinem's *Revolution from Within* (1992) as well as her *Outrageous Acts and Everyday Rebellions* (1983) and *Moving beyond Words* (1994). Heilbrun traces the childhood and adolescence of Steinem, who emerged from a dysfunctional background; she had an irresponsible father and neurasthenic mother who suffered nervous breakdowns and was institutionalized.

As caretaker and nurturer of her mother, Steinem went through a role reversal, which she recounts in "Ruth's Song," written soon after her mother's death in 1981. It is a memoir that might have served in part as catharsis. Born in Toledo, Ohio, in a working-class neighborhood, surrounded by classmates whose futures were practically fixed in amber— they would marry young and languish in dull, low-paying jobs— Steinem determined not to confine herself to the same destiny.

Heilbrun describes Steinem's years at Smith College, in Northampton, Massachusetts, when she associated with the daughters of affluent families and felt her own economic deprivation. Unlike many Smith graduates, Steinem took "the road less traveled" by declining to marry and have children, instead creating her own "narrative," as Heilbrun often terms such independence. Steinem determined to spend her junior year in Europe, received a grant for summer study at Oxford, England, and was awarded a postgraduate fellowship for travel in India, an experience that became seminal in the development of her social and feminist psychology. Returning from India, she traveled by way of Burma, Hong Kong, and Japan.

Like most well-educated women in the 1960s, Heilbrun continues, Steinem confronted a severe bias against women in seeking work in her chosen field—journalism. But with the help of people like Clay Felker—for whom she first worked at *Esquire* and then joined at *New York* magazine, which he founded—she launched her journalistic career. Steinem also wrote for *Glamour, Ladies Home Journal, Vogue,* and the *New York Times Magazine.* Many people are familiar with the story of Steinem's going undercover as a "bunny" to write an exposé of the New York Playboy Club.

Familiar, too, are many of Heilbrun's recountings of the assortment of men with whom Steinem had liaisons; Heilbrun's thoroughness in covering this part of Steinem's life nearly gives the impression that Heilbrun is overcompensating for some perception that Steinem might be lesbian. The known terrain of Steinem's support of the candidacy of George McGovern and the struggle of Cesar Chavez, the farm workers' advocate, is also covered.

The chapter "Awakening," after a short but absorbing history of the women's movement, describes Steinem's moment of epiphany in becoming a feminist. "[She] did not," says Heilbrun, "take part in the radical women's movement until she attended the Redstockings' speakout on abortion in 1969" (*EW,* 13). Then Steinem covered a local abortion hearing for *New York,* details of which Heilbrun quotes from Steinem's *Outrageous Acts* (*EW,* 170). From these reference points, Steinem battled tirelessly for the many causes of women. One Steinem article written for *Look* magazine, entitled "Why We Need a Woman President in 1976," written in January 1970, evoked much comment. Heilbrun considers the article an example of "naïveté."

Perhaps Steinem, even today, is well known for her efforts in the founding of *Ms.* magazine and serving as one of several editors from 1972 to 1989, when it was purchased by Australians. Heilbrun, however, doesn't hone in on *Ms.* magazine until well (20 pages) into the chapter. When Heilbrun does discuss the magazine, especially its genesis and feminism, she fleshes out the history with some absorbing details. The magazine began, for instance, with Clay Felker's idea of inserting an expanded version of a Women's Action Alliance newsletter in his *New York* magazine; he and Steinem arranged to include a 30-page section of articles by women around a theme they called "the contagion of feminism." This was to be followed by a preview issue of 100 pages to be published nationally. In spring 1972 the first complete issue of *Ms.* appeared, and in July 1972 the first regular issue of the magazine was launched, with Steinem and Pat Carbine as the leading editors. Heilbrun discusses Steinem's unremitting and tireless efforts for the magazine together with her constant traveling throughout the United States to support the magazine, women, feminism, and any other worthy cause.

In the chapter "Dissonance at Close Quarters" Heilbrun discusses the internecine strife in the many factions of feminism, but especially Betty Friedan's attack on Steinem when the elder feminist—one-time director of the National Organization for Women (NOW) and a founder of the National Women's Political Caucus (NWPC)—was not selected to serve on the caucus steering committee. When Steinem was chosen as the spokesperson for the Democratic convention, Friedan attacked her for "'ripping off the movement'" (*EW,* 240). Heilbrun gives a detailed account of Friedan's combativeness: her attack on lesbianism, her misrepresentation of Steinem and others as "man-haters," and her anger at what she perceived to be her neglect by the media. Yet Heilbrun gives credit to Friedan's influence on the feminist movement with *The Feminine Mystique* and her work in NOW and its legal defense fund. Friedan also attacked *Ms.* frequently for what she saw as the magazine's failure to give her adequate coverage or credit.

Heilbrun writes at length about *Ms.* magazine—its intention to attract women readers from all economic levels, to publish stories in a wide range of ideas about feminism by many different writers (530 were published in the first years of the magazine), and to print thousands of letters from all kinds of women all over the country. In Heilbrun's view, *Ms.* appeared distinctly feminist. "In a world where the media often misrepresents the movement and almost never depicts feminism fairly or without also offering an anti-feminist counter, *Ms.* spoke directly and unapologetically for a clear, feminist point of view" (*EW,* 251). The magazine's difficulty with advertisers, the readers who felt the magazine's articles appealed to the wrong level, and its lack of hierarchical structure all created problems. Some readers will be sobered at Heilbrun's cataloguing of the many vicious, personal attacks on Steinem: for publicity mongering, lesbianism (which she neither practices nor condemns), and greed (although Steinem contributes heavily to many different causes, especially the Women's Action Alliance, as well as gives freely of her energy).

Heilbrun spends much time on these attacks in the chapter "Trashing," especially on the Redstockings' accusations, which cited Steinem in 1975 as a Central Intelligence Agency collaborator/agent/plant to undermine radical women's groups. Heilbrun asserts, "The Redstockings made a very clever move against a woman they perceived as having usurped their movement and the celebrity owed them"

(*EW,* 288). Heilbrun devotes several pages to Friedan's attacks on Steinem in her book *It Changed My Life* (1976) and calls this book a "monument of innuendo" (*EW,* 301). Ultimately, Heilbrun summarizes what she terms Friedan's obsession with Steinem as "most notable for the harm it does to the cause of feminism" (*EW,* 303). It is most curious that, as Heilbrun states, Steinem never publicly assailed Friedan; when Steinem herself was attacked, she replied only marginally to specific allegations.

When Steinem reached her fiftieth year, she seemed exhausted from all the traveling, speaking, and talk show appearances, especially in publicizing her *Outrageous Acts and Everyday Rebellions.* Steinem, also, having given money to many causes for women, was not herself financially secure. After psychotherapy she would soon begin to husband her resources—physical, psychic, and economic. Morton Zuckerman, with whom she had one of her more publicized romances, astutely characterized Steinem as a poor businesswoman, possessing "editorial genius but not economic know-how" (*EW,* 361). The chapter "Getting to Fifty," which discusses Steinem's affair with Zuckerman, may interest some readers even though much of Heilbrun's information is taken from Steinem's *Revolution from Within* (though Steinem does not identify him by name). Steinem's explanation for the limitations and the termination of the romance involves their sharp differences in economic and social values and politics and her final acceptance of her inability to change him. Interestingly enough, Zuckerman, with his enormous wealth, was one of the few caretakers among Steinem's many personal involvements. It was a propitious nurturing, because Steinem at this stage of her life was "burned out."

Steinem's psychotherapy, begun when Steinem reached age 52, is explored in "Imperative for Change." For the first time she began to look within and to realize that in her need to change society for the betterment of women and to help other causes, she had neglected herself economically and emotionally. Having lived for most of her life Bohemian style with few amenities, she now began to renovate her apartment and to live with a sense of permanence and comfort.

Heilbrun cites the perceptions that evolved from Steinem's therapy: having had to be a mother to her mother, she thus did not want children of her own; she had become almost obsessed with helping people; she had permitted *Ms.* to have too tenacious a hold on her energies; and she had lacked a desire for material possessions. Heilbrun asserts that in a sense, Steinem had been an adolescent for five decades.

At this juncture, with income from her books and from her job as contributing editor for Random House, Steinem finally, with the help of therapy, found the will and the means to plan and secure her future. In 1992 Steinem resumed her community work by campaigning for women candidates in politics, supporting Anita Hill, and publicizing the problem of sexual harassment.

Heilbrun summarizes and discusses *Revolution from Within* as a book on self-esteem, a quality she sees as essential to individual well-being and political revolution. With self-esteem comes the energy to set aside the haunting past and to shape the future. The critical reception of this book is also documented, including Heilbrun's own somewhat negative reaction to its overemphasis on the effects of childhood. Nonetheless, Heilbrun believes *Revolution from Within* to be "wholly a feminist book."

It is Heilbrun's view that "A comprehensive history of so-called second wave feminism in the last half of the twentieth century has yet to be written" (*EW*, 161) and that forthcoming is a "worldwide backlash against feminism. . . . How to counter this backlash, particularly in the light of its extensive financing [by anti-feminists] and influence on the media, is the major question women the world over will face now" (*EW*, 414). One of the ways that Steinem believes the movement will survive and grow stronger is through women from all "boundaries" speaking to each other—a community of strength.

Finally, Heilbrun believes that despite Steinem's revelations about herself in speeches and books and by so many others in various media, Steinem remains an "enigma," a "paradox." "But to the many thousands she has helped or encouraged or rescued, she is, like the Kilroy of World War II, essential and ubiquitous: Steinem was here" (*EW*, 415).

The critical reaction to *The Education of a Woman* was, perhaps unfairly, mostly negative. Surely, Heilbrun, although she retreads much material already published about Steinem, coordinates, expands, and interprets many aspects of the life and the education of one of today's leading feminists. In "Saint Gloria," published in *New York* magazine, Margaret Talbot derides the book by "the besotted Heilbrun," who presents only laudatory material on Steinem. Talbot believes that Steinem's "most important contribution to the women's movement" was her own image and unfavorably compares Steinem to Betty Friedan and Kate Millett, a movement theorist, and labels *Revolution from Within* "a treacle of familiar pop-psych teachings on self esteem."[15] Heilbrun treats Steinem, continues Talbot, "like a doting mother with a camera, illuminating her darling with a brilliant flash while everything around her fades into soft focus" (59). Finally, Talbot is dissatisfied with Heilbrun's failure to evaluate articles in *Ms.*, concluding with this remark: "And Heilbrun honors Steinem; what she doesn't always honor is the critical intelligence of her reader" (59).

Another reviewer, critic and feminist Wendy Kaminer, in the *New York Times Book Review,* does pay some tribute to Gloria Steinem as she emerges in Heilbrun's book, but she feels that Heilbrun "fails to illuminate what she calls Ms. Steinem's 'elusive' personality. Instead, she tends to take her subject at face value, mirroring the self-image that Ms. Steinem presents in her work." Kaminer rejects Heilbrun's assertion that Steinem's good looks played a lesser part in her career than her ideas. Actually, Kaminer insists, it would be more accurate to say her "looks would not be more significant than her activism."[16] Kaminer believes that Heilbrun does not offer "analysis, much less criticism, of Ms. Steinem's ideas," such as censoring pornography, and that Heilbrun's presentation of Steinem's capacity for empathy may not be a strength, but "it may also contribute to her intellectual weakness." Kaminer concludes that Steinem may have become a symbol for the women's movement by chance but that she remains one by design. "The woman who strode through the past twenty-five years of public life strides, along with the feminist movement, beyond the ken of this tentative, feminine book" (37).

Chapter Seven

Conclusion

From the many speeches she has given, grants and fellowships received, the varied teaching done from coast to coast, together with the many articles and books she has published and the numberless committees and women's groups she has served, Carolyn G. Heilbrun has become a national figure as a professor emerita, scholar, feminist, and detective novelist.

Her work demonstrates an unhesitating courage in the face of male hegemony to destroy its prevailing shibboleths and "sacred" theories. Primarily, her writing validates the study of literature through the frame of feminism, resulting in a fresh perspective on not only her special field of modern British literature but also on other periods, such as the English Renaissance and Victorian literature. She has focused, especially in the last decade, on the biographies of women.

Some critics question her scholarship, her biases, and what they perceive as her failure to develop her ideas. Although Heilbrun does pay respect to some men who have supported her lifelong quest of feminism, especially her husband, she spends little time on men around the country who support women's causes. Lionel Trilling, of course, she alternatively praises for having shared with her his vision of literature and attacks for having excluded feminism from that vision and herself—as a woman and a feminist—from his professional consideration.

Many readers delight in Heilbrun's (and Amanda Cross's) abundant use of quotations, while others find the quotations excessive and distracting. Heilbrun has in many interviews admitted to enjoying the use of well-turned phrases, the wit and wisdom of cultured minds. Heilbrun also alludes hundreds of times to the life and writings of Virginia Woolf, one of the writers—feminist and otherwise—she most admires. She quotes Woolf extensively, to the enjoyment of some readers and the irritation of others.

Carolyn G. Heilbrun has been an inspiration to many feminists. In October 1992 she was honored in a day-long seminar at the Graduate Center of the City University of New York, where dozens of speakers joined her on the podium, including such well-known feminists as Jane

Marcus, Catherine Stimpson, and Alice Jardine. Hundreds came to be part of the tribute paid to Heilbrun for her influence on other scholars and professors and on students. At this symposium, "Out of the Academy and into the World with Carolyn Heilbrun," Columbia University's Department of English and Comparative Literature, from which Heilbrun had just retired, was the butt of severe criticism. At the university Heilbrun stirred controversy, with some colleagues supporting her and others condemning her for her peppery iconoclasm and her charges of ill treatment there because she is a woman.

Nancy K. Miller, professor and writer of books on feminism, says of Heilbrun, "For feminists of my generation . . . it has always seemed that Carolyn Heilbrun was already there, there for us, and yet still somehow ahead. . . . Her language and its resistance to the stereotypes of privilege and comfort keep alive the difference of view that defines the outsider" (*HM,* xiv, xvi). The work of Carolyn Heilbrun, as Miller and other feminists have written, has smoothed the way for women beginning to write their own texts.

Notes and References

Abbreviations used in the text for primary works (listed chronologically in order of publication):

The Garnett Family: GF
Christopher Isherwood: CI
Lady Ottoline's Album: LOA
Toward a Recognition of Androgyny: TRA
Reinventing Womanhood: RW
The Representation of Women in Fiction: RWF
Writing a Woman's Life: WWL
Hamlet's Mother and Other Women: HM
The Education of a Woman: The Life of Gloria Steinem: EW

For the Amanda Cross novels (listed chronologically in order of publication):

In the Last Analysis: LA
The James Joyce Murder: JJM
Poetic Justice: PJ
The Theban Mysteries: TM
The Question of Max: QM
Death in a Tenured Position: DTP
Sweet Death, Kind Death: SD
No Word from Winifred: NWW
A Trap for Fools: TF
The Players Come Again: PCA
An Imperfect Spy: IS

Chapter One

   1. Carolyn G. Heilbrun, *Reinventing Womanhood* (New York and London: W. W. Norton and Co., 1979), 56; hereafter cited in text as *RW.*

   2. Carolyn G. Heilbrun, *Writing a Woman's Life* (New York: Ballantine Books, 1989), 26–27; hereafter cited in text as *WWL.*

   3. Miriam Berkley, "Carolyn Heilbrun/Amanda Cross," *Publishers Weekly,* 14 April 1989, 47; hereafter cited in text.

   4. The quote is taken from William Gibson, *A Season in Heaven* (New York: Atheneum, 1974), 46.

   5. Nancy K. Miller, *Subject to Change: Reading Feminist Writing* (New York: Columbia University Press, 1988), 129. Heilbrun's discussion appears in *Writing a Woman's Life,* 18–19.

    6. Anne Matthews, "Rage in a Tenured Position," *New York Times,* 8
November 1992, 75; hereafter cited in text.
    7. Christina Hoff Sommers, *Who Stole Feminism: How Women Have
Betrayed Women* (New York: Simon & Schuster, 1994), 22–23; hereafter cited in
text.
    8. The books cited are Gloria Steinem, *Revolution from Within* (Boston:
Little, Brown, 1992); Marilyn French, *The War against Women* (New York:
Simon & Schuster, 1992); Susan Faludi, *Backlash: The Undeclared War against
American Women* (New York: Crown, 1991).
    9. Kate Mulligan, "Heilbrunian Adventures," *AARP Bulletin,* February
1996, 16.
    10. Robin Pogrebin, "Woman Scholar Quits Columbia, Charges a
Potemkin Feminist Show," *New York Observer,* 11 May 1993, 25; hereafter cited
in text.
    11. Carolyn Heilbrun, "Silence and Women's Voices," in *Women's Voices,*
ed. Lorna Duphiney Edmundson, Judith P. Saunders, and Ellen S. Silber
(Littleton, Mass.: Copley Publishing Group, 1987), 8–9.

Chapter Two

    1. Carolyn G. Heilbrun, *The Garnett Family* (New York: Macmillan
Co., 1961); hereafter cited in text as *GF.*
    2. *Bookman,* June 1906, 90.
    3. Quoted from Richard Garnett [grandson of Constance and
Edward], *Constance Garnett: A Heroic Life* (London: Sinclair-Stevenson, 1991),
225. And also see Richard Garnett's *De Flagello Myrteo, Three-hundred-sixty
Thoughts and Fancies on Love* (Portland, Me.: Thomas B. Mosher, 1906), IX.
    4. Richard Garnett, *Essays of an Ex-Librarian* (London: W. Heinemann,
1901).
    5. Richard Garnett, *The Twilight of the Gods and Other Tales* (London:
Unwin, 1888).
    6. Richard Ellmann, *James Joyce* (New York: Oxford University Press,
1982), 403–4. Joyce's *Portrait of the Artist as a Young Man* was rejected by
Duckworth's reader Edward Garnett, who thought the book "too discursive,
formless, unrestrained, and ugly things, ugly words, are too prominent." He
advised pruning, restraint, and proportion.
    7. Edward Garnett, *Papa's War and Other Stories* (London: George
Allen and Unwin, 1919).
    8. Edward Garnett, *Turgenev* (London: W. Collins Sons, 1917); noted
by Heilbrun in *GF,* 185. Edward wrote introductions to nine of Constance's
volumes on Turgenev.
    9. Constance Garnett's obituary appeared in the 6 January 1947 issue
of the *New Republic,* 40–41.
    10. Miranda Seymour, *Ottoline Morrell: Life on the Grand Scale* (New
York: Farrar, Straus and Giroux, 1992) 334; hereafter cited in text.

11.   In the chapter "Constance Garnett," Heilbrun relies heavily on David Garnett's three volumes of memoirs, cited in note 12 (following), together with unpublished manuscripts by David Garnett concerning his mother, letters in his possession, an unpublished manuscript Constance Garnett wrote in 1928, and magazine and newspaper articles.

12.   David Garnett, *The Golden Echo* (London: Chatto and Windus, 1953); *The Flowers of the Forest* (London: Chatto and Windus, 1955); *The Familiar Faces* (London: Chatto and Windus, 1962).

13.   David Garnett, *Lady into Fox* (London: Chatto and Windus, 1924).

14.   David Garnett, *Beany-Eye* (London: Chatto and Windus, 1935); *No Love* (London: Chatto and Windus, 1929).

15.   Richard Hoggart, "Chosen Tasks," *New Statesman,* 7 July 1961, 11.

16.   Carolyn G. Heilbrun, *Christopher Isherwood* (New York: Columbia University Press, 1970); hereafter cited in text as *CI.*

17.   John Unterecker, *Lawrence Durrell;* William York Tindall, *W. B. Yeats;* Carl Woodring, *Virginia Woolf.* All from the series Columbia Essays on Modern Writers.

18.   Claude J. Summers, "Christopher Isherwood," in *British Novelists, 1930–1959,* vol. 15 of *Dictionary of Literary Biography,* (Detroit: Gale Research Co., 1983).

19.   *Lady Ottoline's Album,* ed. Carolyn G. Heilbrun (New York: Alfred A. Knopf, 1976); hereafter cited in text as *LOA.*

20.   D. H. Lawrence, *Women in Love* (New York: Viking Press, 1920, 1922).

21.   Michael Holroyd, *Lytton Strachey: A Critical Biography,* (New York: Holt Rinehart, 1968), 2:57–58; hereafter cited in text.

22.   William Plomer, *Recollections of Virginia Woolf,* ed. Joan Russell Noble (New York: William Morrow, 1952), 107.

23.   Virginia Woolf, *To the Lighthouse* (New York: Harcourt Brace Jovanovich, 1949), 78.

24.   Trevor Wilson, *The Downfall of the Liberal Party* (Ithaca: Cornell University Press, 1966), 32.

25.   E. M. Forster, *Two Cheers for Democracy* (New York: Harcourt Brace Jovanovich, 1962), 232–33.

26.   P. N. Furbank, "The Personality of E. M. Forster," *Encounter,* November 1970, 61.

27.   Siegfried Sassoon, *Siegfried's Journey* (New York: Viking Press, 1946), 12.

Chapter Three

1.   Carolyn G. Heilbrun, *Toward a Recognition of Androgyny* (New York: Alfred A. Knopf, 1973). Published in England as *Toward Androgyny* (London: Victor Gollancz, 1973). The edition used in this book is that first published by W. W. Norton in 1982; reissued in 1993; hereafter cited in text as *TRA.*

2. Ian Watts, *The Rise of the Novel* (Berkeley and Los Angeles: University of California Press, 1959).

3. Angus Wilson, *The World of Charles Dickens* (New York: Viking Press, 1970).

4. Winifred Holtby, *Virginia Woolf* (London: Wishart and Co., 1932).

5. Carl Woodring, *Virginia Woolf* (New York: Columbia University Press, 1966), 27.

6. Joyce Carol Oates, "An Imperative to Escape the Prison of Gender," *New York Times Book Review,* 15 April 1973, 7; hereafter cited in text.

7. "Reader's Guide: *Toward a Recognition of Androgyny,*" *Yale Review,* Summer 1973, viii; hereafter cited in text.

8. Bruno Bettelheim, *The Uses of Enchantment* (New York: Vintage Books, 1977), 149.

9. Nancy Chodorow, *The Reproduction of Mothering: Psychoanalysis and the Sociology of Gender* (Berkeley: University of California Press, 1978).

10. Ann Hulbert, "Brief Reviews," *New Republic,* 9 June 1979, 40; hereafter cited in text.

11. Margo Jefferson, "The Lives of Women," *New York Times Book Review,* 13 May 1979, 31.

12. Sara Ruddick, "Book Review," *Harvard Educational Review,* November 1979, 551; hereafter cited in text.

Chapter Four

1. James Hillman, *Revisioning Psychology* (New York: Harper Perennial, 1975), 12.

2. Steven R. Carter, "Amanda Cross," in *Ten Women of Mystery,* ed. Earl F. Bargainnier (Bowling Green, Ohio: Bowling Green State University Press, 1981), 270; hereafter cited in text.

3. Amanda Cross, *In the Last Analysis* (New York: Avon, 1964); hereafter cited in text as *LA.*

4. *Webster's New Collegiate Dictionary,* 150th anniversary edition, s.v. "categorical imperative."

5. Rebecca R. Butler, "Amanda Cross, Carolyn Heilbrun," in *Critical Survey of Mystery and Detective Fiction,* ed. Frank N. Magill (Pasadena: Salem Press, 1988), 426; hereafter cited in text.

6. Diana Cooper-Clark, *Designs of Darkness: Interviews with Detective Novelists* (Bowling Green, Ohio: Bowling Green State University Popular Press, 1983), 200; hereafter cited in text.

7. Amanda Cross, *The James Joyce Murder* (New York: Ballantine Books, 1967), 167; hereafter cited in text as *JJM.*

8. Melvin J. Friedman, "Book Reviews, *The James Joyce Murder,*" *Modern Language Journal* 51, no. 6 (October 1967): 373.

9.   Amanda Cross, *Poetic Justice* (New York: Avon, 1970), 94; hereafter cited in text as *PJ*.

10.   Carol Cleveland, "Amanda Cross," in *Twentieth-Century Crime and Mystery Writers,* ed. Lesley Cross Henderson (New York: St. Martin's Press, 1991), 273.

11.   J. M. Purcell, "The 'Amanda Cross' Case: Sociologizing the U.S. Academic Mystery," *Armchair Detective,* Winter 1980, 38–39; hereafter cited in text.

12.   Amanda Cross, *The Theban Mysteries* (New York: Avon, 1971), 53; hereafter cited in text as *TM*.

13.   Newgate Callendar, "Criminals at Large: *The Theban Mysteries,*" *New York Times Book Review,* 31 October 1971, 30.

14.   Amanda Cross, *The Question of Max* (New York: Ballantine Books, 1976), 19; hereafter cited in text as *QM*.

15.   For Carolyn Heilbrun, Oxford was indeed a sacred spot, since Dorothy L. Sayers attended Somerville College there and taught at the university. Those who have been students or visiting professors at Oxford seem never to forget the dons' lawns and gardens, the climbing roses, the ancient staircases, the scout (tea server and general factotum), the Bodleian Library, the Sheldonian, Blackwell's bookstore, the deer at Magdalen College, and most of all those grey spires and halls of learning, where at open lectures, seminars, and tutorials, sherry is served by the professors, who are usually wearing well-raveled academic gowns.

Chapter Five

1.   Diane Cooper-Clark, "Interview with Amanda Cross," in *Designs of Darkness: Interviews with Detective Novelists* (Bowling Green, Ohio: Bowling Green State University Popular Press, 1983), 202.

2.   Katha Pollitt, "Books in Brief: *Death in a Tenured Position,*" *Mother Jones,* August 1981, 65.

3.   Amanda Cross, *Death in a Tenured Position* (New York: Ballantine Books, 1981), 135; hereafter cited in text as *DTP*.

4.   Patricia Craig, "In the Men's Room," *Times Literary Supplement,* 3 July 1981, 758. In England, *Death in a Tenured Position* was published as *A Death in the Faculty*.

5.   Jeffrey Burke, "Mysteries for the Misbegotten," *Harper's Magazine,* July 1981, 74.

6.   Jean M. White, "Mysteries: *Death in a Tenured Position,*" in *Book World, Washington Post,* 15 March 1981, 6.

7.   John Leonard, "Reflex and *Death in a Tenured Position,*" *New York Times,* 20 March 1981; rpt., *Books of the Times,* June 1981, 252–54.

8.   Amanda Cross, *Sweet Death, Kind Death* (New York: Ballantine Books, 1984), 54; hereafter cited in text as *SD*.

9. "Mystery and Crime," *New Yorker,* 14 May 1984, 151.
10. T. J. Bunyan, "Amanda Cross, *Sweet Death, Kind Death,*" *Times Literary Supplement,* 15 February 1985, 179.
11. Newgate Callendar, "Criminals at Large: *Sweet Death, Kind Death,*" *New York Times Book Review,* 24 June 1984, 41.
12. Amanda Cross, *No Word from Winifred* (New York: Ballantine Books, 1986), 223; hereafter cited in text as *NWW.*
13. Amanda Cross, *A Trap for Fools* (New York: Ballantine Books, 1989), 1; hereafter cited in text as *TF.*
14. Maureen T. Reddy, "The Feminist Counter-Tradition in Crime: Cross, Grafton, Paretsky, and Wilson," in *The Cunning Craft* (Macomb: Yeast Printing, 1990), 186.
15. Amanda Cross, *The Players Come Again* (New York: Ballantine Books, 1990), 223; hereafter cited in text as *PCA.*
16. Amanda Cross, *An Imperfect Spy* (New York: Ballantine Books, 1995), 227; hereafter cited in text as *IS.*
17. Richard Kahlenberg, *Broken Contract: A Memoir of Harvard Law School* (London: Faber and Faber, 1992).
18. For ideas on the psychosocial analysis of Kate Fansler I am deeply indebted to Dr. Maxine Theodoulou, psychologist, semanticist, and a seminar participant in Albert Ellis's rational-emotive therapy.
19. Michael Malone, "The Smoke in the Archives," review of P. D. James's *Original Sin, New York Times Book Review,* 2 April 1995, 11.
20. Review of *The Players Come Again, Publishers Weekly,* 31 August, 1990, 51.

Chapter Six

1. Carolyn Heilbrun and Margaret R. Higonnet, ed., *The Representation of Women in Fiction* (Baltimore and London: Johns Hopkins University Press, 1983); hereafter cited in text as *RWF.*
2. Betty Friedan, *The Fountain of Age* (New York: Simon & Schuster, 1993), 181.
3. As quoted by Carolyn Heilbrun in *WWL,* 16, from Deborah Cameron, *Feminism and Linguistic Theory* (London: Macmillan, 1985), 155–56.
4. Carolyn Heilbrun, "Is Biography Fiction?" *Soundings* 76, no. 2–3 (Summer–Fall 1993): 295–304; hereafter cited in text as "Biography."
5. Phyllis Rose, *Writing on Women: Essays in a Renaissance* (Middletown, Conn.: Wesleyan University Press, 1985), 76–77.
6. Stanley Cavell, *Pursuits of Happiness: The Hollywood Comedy of Remarriage* (Cambridge: Harvard University Press, 1981).
7. Winifred Holtby, *Women and a Changing Civilization* (1935; Chicago: Cassandra Edition, Academy Press, 1978); all quotations from this work are from those quoted by Heilbrun in *WWL.*

8. Letter to the author from Arie De Knecht, 15 January 1995.

9. Wendy Martin, "We Are the Stories We Tell," *New York Times Book Review,* 8 January 1989, 19.

10. Carolyn Heilbrun, *Hamlet's Mother and Other Women* (New York: Ballantine Books, 1990), 3; hereafter cited in text as *HM.*

11. Diane Fortuna, "The Labyrinth as Controlling Image in Joyce's *A Portrait of the Artist as a Young Man,"* *Bulletin of the New York Public Library* 76, no. 124 (1972).

12. Phillipe Sollers, "Joyce & Co.," *Triquarterly,* no. 38 (Winter 1977): 109.

13. Helen Vendler, "Feminism and Literature," *New York Review of Books,* 31 May 1990, 23; hereafter cited in text.

14. Carolyn Heilbrun, *The Education of a Woman: The Life of Gloria Steinem* (New York: Dial Press, 1995), xviii; hereafter cited in text as *EW.*

15. Margaret Talbot, "Saint Gloria," *New York,* 23 October 1995, 58; hereafter cited in text.

16. Wendy Kaminer, "A Virtuous Woman," *New York Times Book Review,* 10 September 1995, 36; hereafter cited in text.

Selected Bibliography

PRIMARY WORKS

Nonfiction Books

Christopher Isherwood. New York: Columbia University Press, 1970.

The Education of a Woman: The Life of Gloria Steinem. New York: Dial Press, 1995.

The Garnett Family. New York: MacMillan Co., 1961; London: Allen and Unwin, 1961.

Hamlet's Mother and Other Women. New York: Columbia University Press, 1990. Reprint. New York: Ballantine Books, 1990.

Lady Ottoline's Album. Edited by Carolyn Heilbrun. New York: Knopf, 1976; London: Michael Joseph, 1977.

Reinventing Womanhood. New York: W. W. Norton and Co., 1979. London: Victor Gollancz, 1979. Reprint. Norton paperback, 1981.

The Representation of Women in Fiction. Edited by Carolyn G. Heilbrun and Margaret R. Higgonet. Baltimore and London: Johns Hopkins University Press, 1983.

Toward a Recognition of Androgyny: Aspects of Male and Female in Literature. New York: Knopf, 1973. Published in England as *Toward Androgyny.* London: Victor Gollancz, 1973. Reprint. New York. Harper Torchbook, 1975. New York: W. W. Norton, 1982.

Writing a Woman's Life. New York: W. W. Norton, 1988. Reprint. New York: Ballantine Books, 1989.

Amanda Cross Detective Novels

Death in a Tenured Position. New York: E. P. Dutton, 1981. Printed in England, as *A Death in the Faculty.* London: Gollancz, 1981. Reprint. New York: Ballantine Books, 1982, 1990.

An Imperfect Spy. New York: Ballantine Books, 1995.

In the Last Analysis. New York: Macmillan Co., 1964. Reprint. New York: Avon Books, 1966.

The James Joyce Murder. New York: Macmillan Co., 1967. Reprint. New York: Ballantine, 1982.

No Word from Winifred. New York: E. P. Dutton, 1986. Reprint. New York: Ballantine Books, 1987.

The Players Come Again. New York: Ballantine Books, 1990.

Poetic Justice. New York: Knopf, 1970. Reprint. New York: Avon Books, 1979.
The Question of Max. New York: Knopf, 1976. Reprint. Ballantine Books, 1984.
Sweet Death, Kind Death. New York: E. P. Dutton, 1984. Reprint. New York: Ballantine Books, 1985, 1991.
The Theban Mysteries. London: V. Gollancz, 1972. Reprint. New York: Avon Books, 1979.
A Trap for Fools. New York: E. P. Dutton, 1989. Reprint. New York: Ballantine Books, 1990, 1992.

Articles and Essays

"Biography between the Lines." In *Dorothy L. Sayers: The Centenary Celebration,* 1–13. New York: Walker and Co., 1993. Reprinted from *American Scholar* 51, no. 4 (Autumn 1992). Heilbrun acknowledges her debt to Sayers and comments on the James Brabazon biography of Sayers, commissioned by her heirs. Finds the biography compelling but laments its neglect of Sayers's feminism.
"Feminist Criticism in Departments of Literature." *Academe* 69, no. 5 (September–October 1983): 11–14. Shows how the bias against the use of feminist criticism is pervasive, a theme that reflects the rigidity of the patriarchy, still dominant in the academy. Contains many valuable insights.
"Is Biography Fiction?" *Soundings* 76, no. 2–3 (Summer–Fall 1993): 295–304. An excellent article on the creativity and interpretation of data involved in writing biography.
"The May Sarton I Have Known." In *Essays and Speeches from the National Conference "May Sarton at 80: A Celebration of Her Life and Work,"* edited by Constance Hunting, 3–12. Orono, Me.: Puckerbrush Press, 1994. Heilbrun praises Sarton's androgynous views as expressed in her literature and her lifestyle, her integrity in not catering to mainstream critics, and her openness in seeing many possibilities in the ways women can live their lives.
———. "Silence and Women's Voices." *Women's Voices* (1987): 4–11. The silence of women may often be thunderous; Heilbrun writes of many silent women in fiction, made mute literally or figuratively.

SECONDARY WORKS

Books, Parts of Books, and Articles

Bunyan, T. J. "Amanda Cross, *Sweet Death, Kind Death.*" *Times Literary Supplement,* 15 February 1985, 179. This British review finds this Cross book absorbing reading, balanced and well-written.
Burke, Jeffrey. "Mysteries for the Misbegotten." *Harper's Magazine,* July 1981, 74. Praises the psychological insight in the solving of the puzzle in *Death in a Tenured Position.*

Butler, Rebecca R. "Amanda Cross, Carolyn G. Heilbrun." *Critical Survey of Mystery and Detective Fiction* (1988): 425–30. This probing article discusses a number of the Cross mysteries. Butler especially applauds the character of Kate Fansler.

Callendar, Newgate. "Criminals at Large: *Sweet Death, Kind Death.*" *New York Times Book Review,* 24 June 1984, 41. The writer's praise of the novel is offset by the archness of tone, and the review is finally deflating.

————. "Criminals at Large: *The Theban Mysteries.*" *New York Times Book Review,* 31 October 1971, 30. Captures the right tone of the novel with the words "quiet and thoughtful."

Carter, Steven R. "Amanda Cross." In *Ten Women of Mystery,* edited by Earl F. Bargainnier, 270–96. Bowling Green, Ohio: Bowling Green State University Press, 1981. This is a lengthy article, excellent in its analysis of the Cross novels, ending with *Death in a Tenured Position,* the seventh novel.

Cleveland, Carol. "Amanda Cross." *Twentieth Century Crime and Mystery Writers* (1991): 273. A most readable article on *Poetic Justice;* echoes the criticism of many—that there may be too many Auden quotations in this mystery.

Craig, Patricia. "In the Men's Room." *Times Literary Supplement,* 3 July 1981, 758. The British review of *Death in a Tenured Position* hones in on the very center of the novel.

Ellman, Richard *James Joyce.* New York: Oxford University Press, 1982, 403–4. These pages are worth reading; the myopia of a British publishing-house reader is amusing in hindsight.

Friedan, Betty. *The Fountain of Age.* New York: Simon & Schuster, 1993. Valuable book by the well-known feminist discussing aging, a theme Heilbrun pursues in books and articles.

Garnett, Richard. *Constance Garnett: A Heroic Life.* London: Sinclair-Stevenson, 1991. Written by Constance Garnett's grandson, who had access to family papers, this book gives a fuller and more personal account of the Russian translator's life than does Heilbrun's *The Garnett Family.* Interesting personal portraits of several of the family's literary acquaintances, including John Galsworthy, Joseph Conrad, and D. H. Lawrence.

Hillman, James. *Revisioning Psychology.* New York: Harper Perennial, 1975. Hillman is difficult to read with his high level of abstraction, but there are many profound insights into the human psyche.

Hulbert, Ann. "Brief Reviews." *New Republic,* 9 June 1979, 40. This review of *Reinventing Womanhood* does the book little justice.

Jefferson, Margo. "The Lives of Women." *New York Times Book Review,* 13 May 1979, 31. This gifted writer's provocative article on *Reinventing Womanhood* and *Toward a Recognition of Androgyny* is required reading, if only for her noting of Heilbrun's contradictory statements on Lionel Trilling. Jefferson also deplores Heilbrun's practice of presenting often-quoted ideas as "radical originality."

Kaminer, Wendy. "A Virtuous Woman." *New York Times Book Review*, 10
     September 1995, 36–37. This review of *The Education of a Woman: The
     Life of Gloria Steinem* is a clear and short summary of the book; notes
     Heilbrun's uncritical approach to her subject.
Malone, Michael. "The Smoke in the Archives." Review of P. D. James's
     Original Sin. New York Times Book Review, 2 April 1995, 11. A stimulating
     article that prods the reader to compare Heilbrun and James.
Martin, Wendy. "We Are the Stories We Tell." *New York Times Book Review*, 8
     January 1989, 19. Enthusiastic article that is notable for its unadulter-
     ated high praise of *Writing a Woman's Life*, which Martin recommends as
     required reading for women before they reach the age of 21.
Oates, Joyce Carol. "An Imperative to Escape the Prison of Gender." *New York
     Times Book Review*, 15 April 1973, 7. This provocative response to *Toward
     a Recognition of Androgyny*, though tepid in praise, is well balanced. Oates
     finds Heilbrun's definition of *androgyny* ambiguous and her discussion of
     some literary characters overlong. She also cites failure to discuss writers
     such as Margaret Drabble and Iris Murdoch, who explore the theme of
     androgyny in their fiction.
Pogrebin, Robin. "Woman Scholar Quits Columbia, Charges a Potemkin Show."
     New York Observer, 11 May 1993, 1, 25. A lively article about the contro-
     versy Heilbrun stirred with her early retirement. Informative and readable.
Pollitt, Katha. "Books in Brief: *Death in a Tenured Position.*" *Mother Jones*, August
     1981, 65. Pollitt was graduated from Harvard, and this fact becomes the
     focus of her article. She cheers Heilbrun's attack on the sexism at her
     alma mater, but finds Heilbrun to be more effective as feminist than as
     mystery writer.
Purcell, J. M. "The 'Amanda Cross' Case: Sociologizing the U.S. Academic
     Mystery." *Armchair Detective* (Winter 1980): 36–40. An excellent article
     with many penetrating insights.
"Reader's Guide." *Yale Review* 62, no. 4 (Summer 1973): viii, x. An acerbic
     review of *Toward a Recognition of Androgyny* that reflects a bias against
     women. It is worth reading to ponder the validity of the writer's claims
     that hormones may be the basis of androgynous behavior.
"Review of *The Players Come Again*." *Publishers Weekly*, 31 August 1990, 51–52.
     This brief review finds ideas rather than plot to be effective.
Ruddick, Sara. "Book Review." *Harvard Educational Review* (November 1979):
     549–55. An in-depth article that discusses the themes in *Reinventing
     Womanhood*, including women as heroes, women's consciousness raising,
     the partial usefulness of male models, and the need for economic empow-
     erment and, above all, for independence.
Seymour, Miranda. *Ottoline Morrell: Life on the Grand Scale*. New York: Farrar,
     Straus and Giroux, 1992. A superb book that shows Morrell—also the
     subject of a book edited by Heilbrun—to be a fascinating figure. The
     Bloomsbury group comes into sharp focus.

Sommers, Christina Hoff. *Who Stole Feminism? How Women Have Betrayed Women.* New York: Simon & Schuster, 1994, esp. 22–23. Written by a philosopher, this controversial book should be read to obtain a balanced view of feminism. Gender feminists and equity feminists are carefully discussed.

Talbot, Margaret. "Saint Gloria." *New York,* 23 October 1995, 58–59. Provides a short, incisive account of feminism before evaluating Heilbrun's biography of Gloria Steinem. Like many critics, finds that Heilbrun practically canonizes Steinem (hence the title). Succinct and well-written.

Vendler, Helen. "Feminism and Literature." *New York Review of Books,* 31 May 1990, 19–22. Finds fallacies throughout *Hamlet's Mother,* especially in Heilbrun's assertion that the language of men as used by all has undermined women. Claims language is a potent force in anyone who is articulate, whether male or female, Shakespeare or Austen. Denounces the "feminist teaching" of literature as defined by Heilbrun in what Vendler calls a book of "moral propaganda." Scholarly and penetrating.

White, Jean M. "Mysteries: *Death in a Tenured Position.*" *Washington Post,* 15 March 1981, 6. Enjoyable article, written with zest and ebullience, yet probes the novel thoughtfully.

Interviews

Berkley, Miriam, "Carolyn Heilbrun/Amanda Cross." *Publishers Weekly,* 14 April 1989, 47–48. Covers much of Heilbrun's background and reflections on her detective novels.

Cooper-Clark, Diana. "Interview with Amanda Cross." *Designs of Darkness: Interviews with Detective Novelists,* 187–202. Bowling Green, Ohio: Bowling Green State University Popular Press, 1983. Cooper-Clark and Heilbrun cover many facets of detective novels, with Amanda Cross enumerating her favorite mystery writers. Informative.

Lussier, Mark, and Peggy McCormack. "Heilbrun: An Interview." *New Orleans Review* 13, no. 3 (1986): 65–73. Valuable article. Discussion ranges from politics and literary criticism to men and feminist theory. Highly recommended.

Matthews, Anne. "Rage in a Tenured Position." *New York Times,* 8 November 1992, 47, 72–73, 75, 83. Although much of the article favors Heilbrun's position in her dramatic departure from Columbia, Matthews has made an attempt to obtain other views.

Letter

De Knecht, Arie, to the author, 15 January 1995. Mr. De Knecht writes a critique of *Writing a Woman's Life* and, a feminist himself, finds Heilbrun's book off-putting and imbalanced for failure to include men who have fostered feminism.

Videocassette

"Out of the Academy and into the World with Carolyn Heilbrun." Day-long
    seminar at City University Graduate School, New York, in honor of
    Carolyn Heilbrun, 30 October 1992. Seven-hour video records literary
    and other luminaries from the disciplines of history, sociology, philoso-
    phy, and more, discussing feminism and giving accolades to Heilbrun.
    Leading feminists such as Nancy K. Miller (*The Heroine's Text*), Sandra
    Gilbert and Susan Gubar (*The Madwoman in the Attic*), Catherine
    Stimpson (*Women's Studies in the United States*), and Deidre Bair (*Simone de
    Beauvoir*) make for interesting viewing and listening.

Index

NONFICTIONAL PROSE

The Author

Julia B. Boken is a professor at the State University of New York, College at Oneonta. She has a Ph.D. in English and comparative literature from Columbia University and a master's degree from the university's Graduate School of Journalism. She has published essays on Simone de Beauvoir, V. S. Pritchett, Jules Hardouin-Mansart, and southern mystery writer Margaret Maron.

The Editor

Frank Day is a professor of English and head of the English Department at Clemson University. He is the author of *Sir William Empson: An Annotated Bibliography* (1984) and *Arthur Koestler: A Guide to Research* (1985). He was a Fulbright lecturer in American literature in Romania (1980–81) and in Bangladesh (1986–87).